The Real Estate Agent
Theoretical Fundament

Written by:

Franklin Díaz

ISBN: 9798842589524
Sello: Independently published
"The Real Estate Agent"
Written By Franklin Díaz
Copyright © 2022 Franklin Díaz
All rights reserved
Special edition for publication in all Amazon portals worldwide in softcover paper format

In memoriam matris meae: Maria Lárez

INDEX

CHAPTER 1: 11

THE REAL ESTATE AGENT. CONCEPT AND GENERALITIES. 11

CHAPTER 2 31

MAIN JURIRIDAL BUSINESS THAT CAN BE DONE WITH THE PROPERTY RIGHTS THAT FALL UPON REAL STATES 31

    1. - SALE 33

    2. - LEASING: 37

    3.- EXCHANGE: 38

    4. - COMODATE OR LOAN OF USE: 39

    5. - DONATION: 40

    6. - MORTGAGE: 41

CHAPTER 3 43

THE REAL ESTATE AGENT AS A NATURAL PERSON 43

CHAPTER 4 53

THE REAL ESTATE AGENT AS A JURIDICAL PERSON 53

    1) COMMERCIAL NAME AND SLOGAN 56

    2) THE SELECTION OF ENTREPRICE TYPE 57

    3) THE CONSTITUTIVE DOCUMENT 58

4) COMMERCIAL HEADQUARTERS	59
ANNEXE I	61
MODEL OF ANNONYMOUS SOCIETY CONSTITUTIVE DOCUMENT	61
ANNEXE II	95
MODEL OF CONSTITUTIVE DOCUMENT OF A SOCIETY OF LIABILITY LIMITED (L.L.S)	95
CHAPTER 5	113
THE SATE AGENT JOB, ATRIBUTIONS AND FUNCTIONS	113
CHAPTER 6	127
CUSTOMERS PORTFOLIO	127
CLIENTS TYPOLOGY	129
1. - SELLERS:	130
2. - LESSORS	131
3. - PURCHASER	137
4. - LESSEE OR HOUSEHOLDERS	137
CHAPTER 7	139
METHODS OF CLIENTS ATTRACTION	139
PRESS: ADVERTISING IN NEWSPAPERS	141
LEAFLEATS AND FLYERS	143
INTERPERSONAL RELATIONSHIPS	145
INTERNET: AN OPEN WINDOW TO THE WORLD OF THE IMMOVABLE PROPERTY BUSSINESS	147

"PURE AND HARD" SALES TECHNIQUE: THE "COLD DOOR" SELLER" 151

MEETING THE HUMANS 155

CHAPTER 8 159

MARKETING TECHNIQUES 159

   1. - LOVE FOR SELLING 160

   2. - KNOWLEDGE OF THE PRODUCT TO SELL 163

   3. - KEEP UP TO DATE WITH THE PRICES OF THE IMMOVABLE TRADING 165

   4. - BE ONESELF 166

   5. - SINCERE GREETING AND CORDIAL SMILE 167

   6. - ATTRACT ATTENTION, INTEREST AND DESIRE: 168

   7. - PRONOUNCE THE NAME OR SURNAME OF THE CLIENT FREQUENTLY. 171

   8. - BE EFFECTIVE LISTENER 171

   9. - WE MUST BE CONSCIOUS OF OUT LIMITS 173

   10. - WE HAVE TO ADMIT VALID OBJECTIONS. 174

   11. - DO NOT USE THE EXPRESSION: "YES, BUT…" 175

   12. - CLOSING RECOMMENDATIONS 176

CHAPTER 9 181

THE EARNINGS: THE FRUIT OF STATE AGENT LABOR 181

   SALES 183

   LEASSING: 184

FINAL CONSIDERATION OF THE SECOND PART OF THIS BOOK 187

CHAPTER 1:

THE REAL ESTATE AGENT. CONCEPT AND GENERALITIES

The estate agent is a person, natural or juridical, that operates in his own name or representation of others, mediating between people who wish to make a juridical business with a real estate.

It is necessary to establish some precisions regarding this concept.

In the first place, it is important to clear out that when we consider a person "natural" or "juridical" we mean that it can be a person, such as a human being, or an enterprise. Both are "persons" from the legal point of view, and as a consequence, they are holders of rights and obligations. The first of them are considered "natural persons", and the second are "juridical persons".

In the second place, the expression "in his own name o representing others" means that the operation can be done by the agent by himself, or as an emissary or agent of other person.

When we say that the agent acts "in his own name", we refer that he operates on his behalf, that is to say, without representing anybody but himself, like an individual. On the contrary, when we say that the agent operates in representation of other, in this case his operations are made on behalf of a third person, natural or juridical.

It seems simple at first sight, but it is important to establish the difference due to the determination of the people who are, or will be, subjected to obligations with the intermediation of the state. When the state acts in his own name, it is obvious that he contracts obligation individually, but, when he does on other people behalf (people or enterprise) the other people are forced to meet their obligations, not him.

Let's explain this point a bit more.

An obligation is a juridical legal bond that joins one person to another. The tenant of an apartment is bound with the leaseholder to pay him the rental fees, to comply with the stipulations of the neighborhood, to keep up with the services which has assumed to pay, and not to deteriorate the property that he has been trusted for its use. These are examples of obligations.

Another example of obligation would be the case in which the property purchaser that asks the Bank for a loan to pay for it. He will be obliged with the bank, during the period stipulated by contract, to pay, in time and form, the amount according to the capital charge-off plus interests.

An example of an incurred obligation by The Real Estate Agent would be when he agrees with the property owner to look for a purchaser or leaseholder according to the previous established conditions.

The breach of this obligation would take place when the owner could demand responsibilities to The Real Estate Agent. Let's suppose that an owner trusts his property to a state agent through a contract, with the requirement that he could rent it only to a couple without children or pets, but The Real Estate Agent leaves that requirement aside and rents it to a numerous family, with four children, two grandparents, an uncle and aunt, dogs, cats and parrots, and even more, they leave the property deteriorated when moving at the end of the contract.

Independently of the tenant's responsibility with the property owner, here comes a responsibility on the part of The Real Estate Agent. He could be demanded by the owner for contract breach, and he will have to face the consequences and damages derived from his own misbehavior. The breach of his obligation caused damage, and to the law "Anyone who causes damage to another person is forced to repair it". This is a universal principle of Law.

If in this concrete case, The Real Estate Agent acts in his own name, he will have to assume personally the consequences of his own acts. Furthermore, if The Real Estate Agent acts in name of a third person, that person will have to assume the responsibility of the obligation breach.

Let's clear now the meaning of "juridical business"

That concept means a pact or agreement made between two or more parts, whose purpose is to produce consequences and legal effects.

Any person that would not be affected by legal limitations can make pacts or agreements to produce juridical effects, in other words; they can contract. Examples of limited people to sign contracts are children and mental disables, among others.

A contract is an agreement between two parts to produce legal consequences. It is a way of creating laws, if you take verbatim, that is to say: "contract is law between the parts". The contractors must respect the contract in the same way they respect the rest of law. The clauses, or parts of a contract, are juridical norms of forced breach to those intervenient people. As long as such clauses do not contradict what is arranged in the valid juridical ordeal. For example, a leasing contract would not be valid if it is stipulated that the hired house has to be exclusively used for selling drugs, prostitution, or any other activity forbidden by law.

Finally, and it is also very important, to clear out what it must be understood by a "real state".

Firstly we must define what they are. What is a "good of property"?

A "good of property" is an object or something that has utility, and it is susceptible of being economically valued. This is the conception.

There are many classifications of properties. The one we are interested in is the classification that splits them into "movable" and "immovable" properties.

What are the immovable properties?

A simple notion tells us that they are the ones that cannot be moved from one place to another without losing its essence, or substance.

You cannot take a house from one place to another without destroying it (unless it is a van, of course). You cannot move the land. You could not take an apartment from one building and put it into another.

The immovable properties are also called "real state", because they are adhered to the soil, tied to the floor with a root, like trees.

And ... What are the movable properties?

On the contrary, movable properties are the ones that can be translated from place to place without losing their essence.

A television set is still a television set even though you take it from the store to your house, unless it falls and breaks on your way home.

So, which are the immovable properties and which are the movable ones?

The "immovable" properties are houses, buildings, apartments, land and farms. On the contrary the "movable" ones are furniture (sofa, armchairs, and chairs), the home appliances (televisions, irons, radios, computers, etc.), beds, dining rooms, bookshelves, etc.

Vehicles, such as cars, auto motors and ships of all classes (ship, yacht, motorboats, etc) are also considered movable properties including spaceships (planes, rockets, etc.). These are different from the rest of movable properties because of their expensive economical value. For that reason they have an exclusive and special registration regime (Automotive Registry for the vehicles; Ships and Aircraft Registry for airplanes; Merchant Marine Registry for the Ships, etc.) It is said that they are a kind of "Movable properties that are used to being registered".

There are also special kinds of movable properties that are considered immovable by the law due to its nature. That is the case of the furniture adhered to a house or apartment, like the cooker or the sanitary or electric facilities, they are considered immovable because of its function.

Which is the importance of this difference?

The most transcendental element as regard the consideration of the property like a movable or unmovable consists above whom the law assists in the process of testing who the right holders are in a determined point in time, that is to say, who the legal owners are, or who the legitimated people are in order to use them.

The owner is the person who appears in this condition in a specific Registry of the rights above the immovable properties or real states.

As regards of the movable properties, the owner is the person who has got the real possession of it, the one who holds it materially, with the exception of the movable properties mentioned above.

There is no Registry to look for the owner of a television, a telephone, or e console, because this registry does not exist.

It is said that in the case of the movable property, the possession is equivalent to the title. That is to say, the person who has got it is the right holder of the property, except somebody can prove the contrary, obviously. A thief cannot be considered the right holder of my mobile telephone only because he has got it, for the simple fact that he has got it materially, he is a person who stole it and took it for him improperly. That is the reason it is said "unless somebody can prove the contrary".

There are some rights on properties, any of them. What are these rights?

The rights are abstract entities, creation of the human mind. They are a kind of "idea". They are not objects that can be touched, like a chair or a glass, but ways of appreciating reality. ¿What is it like? Here come some explanations of it.

Human beings appreciate the world around them through the ideas, the notions that are mere concepts. There are abstract and concrete concepts. For example a chair is a concrete concept. When it is thought of a chair without looking at one, it comes to mind the notion of an object with four legs with a place to sit on it and a back-plate. This is something concrete. But when it is thought in a right, it does not come to the mind a concrete object, that can be described, but an "idea", a notion that can be conceptualized only through determined characteristics. This is an abstract concept.

It is not the same the right in itself or the property upon it relapses. They are two things very different. One thing is a house, and another very different is the right of property on it. It is very important to take into account this difference. Here it is an example.

A person buys a mobile telephone at a store. He takes it to the supermarket and he leaves it forgotten on a shelf.

Question:

Where is the telephone?

Answer:

On the shelf.

Question:

Where is the right of property upon the moblle?

Answer:

The absent minded buyer has got it.

If a third person finds the mobile and takes it to his house, he does not take the right of property with him, but only the mobile, that it is not the same.

Hey? What is it like?

So…? Where is the right? Is it in the pocket of the buyer? Is it part of the mobile? No. None of the answers are correct.

The right of property upon the mobile is in the buyer's mind. It is a personal own idea. But it is not just a simple idea and that is it. It is a kind of appreciation of the reality that can prove. An abstract idea to which the laws attribute validity and juridical effectiveness, and in a certain way, they prove their own existence.

Somebody could tell that the right is in the invoice issued by the seller, but it is not true and we can demonstrate it. The invoice, or the receipt of a purchase, is only the proof of the existence of the right, but not the right in itself.

If it were this way, when the invoice or receipt lost, we would lose the right, and it is not either this way.

If the buyer loses the invoice or the receipt of the purchase, the only thing to do is to go to the store where the mobile was bought and ask for a copy. And if the store cannot give it to him because they have closed up or they have lost it themselves, he could go to look for another type of proof to demonstrate the existence of the right, like witnesses, for example.

As it can be seen, the rights are abstract entities, as it was said at the beginning. They are conceptions of human mind to which the laws provide proper existence, autonomous, independent, and that conveys determined kind of faculties to their holders.

These "rights" we are talking about, cannot exist by themselves, unbounded from the owner. You cannot watch them walking around, like you watch a person or an animal doing so (Unless you are psychiatric)

All the rights fall on property goods. That is to say: every property good belongs to somebody, to a person. There is no property good, as it is understood, that anyone has no right upon it.

Again: All the property goods, movable or immovable, have rights upon them whose anyone is declared as its owner.

People do not have "property goods" in the strict sense, but "rights" upon them.

Is a diamond stone still not discovered anyone's property? The answer is "no", because it is not even considered a good as such. As it has already been said above, for an object to be considered a "good", it must have a utility and it must be susceptible of pecuniary value.

How can an unfound diamond have utility? That would be like to be in love with someone unknown. When someone finds the diamond it would be considered a useful object and it will be susceptible of economical value. Till then it will only be a stone among hundreds of thousands of millions that exist on earth.

The rights upon the goods, according to the conception we are dealing here, give "faculties" to whom they have got them.

The owner will have the faculty depending on the right he has upon the object.

The owner of a house has no the same faculties upon it than its leaser.

Which are the faculties that attribute rights to its holders? They are only three. Namely:

1. - The right of use.

2. - The right of usufruct.

3. - The right of abuse.

Besides they are considered "faculties", in fact they are simultaneously "rights". Let's define them.

The right of use, as its name says, is the one that attributes the holder the faculty to use the good; to make use of it.

The owner of a house or an apartment has the right to use it, but he can temporally give to another person through a contract, that would be in this case a leaseholder.

In this case, the owner would lose temporally the right of use meanwhile the leasing contract lasts. The owner would not use the property, although it is of his own, during the validity of the contract. The owner has transferred the right of use to another person.

The right of usufruct is the right of perceiving the fruits that the good produces.

In the previous example, the owner of the house or apartment in question has the right to perceive the fruits of it, in this case, the rental fees. These are the fruits. He can also give this right to a third person, to his leaseholder, allowing him to sub-rent the immovable property.

Finally, the right of abuse, that is to say that it is the right to do with the good whatever you want.

The owner of the house or apartment in this condition can do what he wants with it, the only limit is law. If it is about a house, he could paint it with fluorescent colors, put a roof made of glass, change the distribution of the interior space, or even destroy it totally or partially if he wishes. But if it is about an apartment, he could not destroy it because it is adhered to a building.

To do everything that feels like is not an expression that must be taken literally. It has its limits in those things that are forbidden by law. An owner of a house cannot change the façade of a house if it is forbidden by a town hall disposition. That is the case of some houses with facades that are considered of historical or cultural interest.

There are other rights upon the goods, like mortgage or pledge, that are also contracts, which attribute to the owners the facully of disposing them in case of no paying a principal obligation. We will talk about it later.

Once cleared these explanations, we can say that we will focus our study on the so called "real states" (building, houses, flats, apartments, farms, lands), and the rights that fall upon them, in the different kinds of juridical business that we can do with them, and in the sales technique and purchasing. These are the subjects we will study.

We can do different types of "juridical business" with the "rights" that we have upon the immovable properties. We do not do transactions with these property goods, but with the "rights" that fall upon them.

We have to make a difference between our ordinary sayings and what actually happens. For example, when we go to a Café, we do not ask the attendant to give us the property right upon a cup of coffee to exercise the right of use and abuse upon it. We simply ask for a cup of coffee, or to sell some coffee to us. But what it is really happening is the first, the less he can be considered is nuts, goofy or in any case a fool.

However, it is very important to have these notions very clear for those people who can dedicate to this activity. It is useful to understand very well every twists and turns of the underworld of the real estate business.

If you have not understood well what you have read up to now, read everything again once more; the number of times you need till you have it fully assimilated. It is only a suggestion that later you will thank to me.

Did you do it? So let's go on

CHAPTER 2

MAIN JURIRIDAL BUSINESS THAT CAN BE DONE WITH THE PROPERTY RIGHTS THAT FALL UPON REAL STATES

The main juridical business we can do with the rights that fall upon Real Sates are:

1. - Sale.
2. - Leasing.
3. - Exchanging.
4. - Comodate or loan of use.
5. - Donation.
6. - Mortgage.

FRANKLIN DÍAZ

1. - SALE

It is a contract by means of which a person called "seller" has to transfer to another called "buyer", THE PROPERTY RIGHT upon an immovable property in exchange of an amount of money.

As it can be appreciated at the beginning of this chapter, property goods are not transferred, but the rights upon them, in this case the property right. Juridical business are not done with the goods such as they really are, but with the rights upon them. This is something we always have to keep in mind.

So: What is the property right?

The property right is the one that attributes the holder all the faculties that can be exerted upon a good. It is the only rights of all that falls upon the good, that gives to the holder all the faculties that can be exerted upon it, We have already learned that these faculties are the right of use, the right of usufruct and the right of abuse.

The holder of the property right can only make this juridical business. Although it seems obvious, it is somewhat complex in certain assumptions. First, it is the determination of the ownership of the right. Who is the holder of the property right upon an immovable good? How can we know?

If you have read carefully the previous chapter, you have already understood that the holder of the property right upon an immovable property is the one that appears in the property Registration of immovable properties.

Pero esto no siempre es así. Se nos pueden presentar algunas situaciones complejas que bien vale la pena analizar.

But it is not always this way. There are some complex situations that are worth of analysis.

The first problem we can face is that the immovable property is not registered. What can we do in such cases?

The seller must solve this situation. The seller hast to register the immovable property under his name if he wants to sell it. It is not advisable to do business with a good without being registered. The registration is the only quality that gives confidence to the purchaser and The Real Estate Agent about the property to be transferred belongs to the person who says to be the owner. That is precisely the reason of existence of that registration of the immovable properties; to inspire trust in the juridical traffic of rights upon them.

In second place, we can also find the situation of an immovable property that not only has a holder, but many. It is useless to say that all of them must be willing to sell the property in order to do the negotiation.

If it is an inherited good it can be sold once the inheritors decide to do the partition of the inheritance community. May be that the property is part of a conjugal community, or a commercial society. In all these cases, there must be expressed authorization from all the co-owners for the property can be sold.

Finally, we must say that we can also find the situation in which the immovable property to negotiate was subjected to a right of mortgage. In this case the property good could be sold if it were freed from the mortgage right, or if it were authorized by the right holder of the mortgage. The property good can only be sold if any of the contracting parts gives their authorization. On the contrary, Can you imagine the purchaser's face when he finds out that he apartment or house he bought is mortgaged?

Besides, it is very important to say that the seller receives an amount of money (not other thing) in exchange of the transference of the property right. Because we would be talking about other type of juridical business rather than a sale in that case.

2. - LEASING:

Leasing or Rent is a contract by means of which a person transfers to another the RIGHT OF USE upon a determined immovable property, in exchange of a fee payment.

Only the person who has got the holding of a right can transfer it. Although it sounds obvious, we bring it up with the purpose of explaining the following.

Firstly, the right of use upon a determined good belongs exclusively to the holder of the property right. But it is not necessary to be always this way. A third person, who is not holder of the property right, could transfer the right of use upon de property good. This is the leaseholder that has been previously authorized by the owner to sub-rent. It is also the case of who has been left the good for its use and enjoy it beyond its limits.

3.- EXCHANGE:

Este contrato es conocido vulgarmente como trueque.

It is a contract by means of which any of both contracting parts are obliged to transfer to another the PROPERTY RIGHT upon a good.

4. - COMODATE OR LOAN OF USE:

It is a contract by means of which a person transfers to another the RIGHT OF USE upon a determined immovable property, without the mediation of any kind of benefit.

That is to say, this is a contract by means of which a person gives another the right of using a determined immovable property without a payment in exchange. Free.

5. - DONATION:

It is a contract by means of which a person transfers the RIGHT OF PROPERTY upon an immovable property to another, free, that is to say, without any payment in exchange.

6. - MORTGAGE:

It is a contract in which it is constituted a right in favor of a third one to guaranty the payment of a main obligation. It is said that it is a subordinated right to the payment of a main obligation, which it depends upon. Once the payment is made, the obligation expires and so does the mortgage.

It is important because if the debtor does not pay his obligations, the holder of the mortgage right can make it execute judicially, asking to a court the auction of the mortgaged property good.

FRANKLIN DÍAZ

CHAPTER 3

THE REAL ESTATE AGENT AS A NATURAL PERSON

Anyone, without any legal limitations from underage or mental condition, can dedicate himself to the business of real state intermediation. No academic degree is necessary. Only some fundamental knowledge is required that will increase and improve with the practice, but it is no necessary a university degree.

Obviously that a Bachelor in Business, Economics, Law or similar will provide you with more knowledge on real state world compared to a person that has not such studies. However, what we want to say is that anyone can do it without the limitations implied in other human occupations.

To mention only two cases, we can say that to defend the citizen at a court it is necessary to be a Lawyer, and you cannot operate a patient in an operating theater unless you are a surgeon physician. To mediate between two people in order to do a real states business only good will is required to go ahead.

This statement has its important variations according the country where you are living. We are going to explain this better.

There are some places on earth where citizens can do what they like to earn money. There are many other places in the African or American continents, where anyone can put a basket of fruits on his head and go out to sell them in any street of his town, and nobody will tell him anything. Previous legal requirements are not necessary.

Even more, in the European countries and others called "Developed" countries (Such us Japan, or U.S.A.), if they find somebody selling fruit with a basket on his head, he will be punished and forbidden to do so, because the human activities for a living are strictly organized and regulated.

In most cases it is not a about the absence of normative, but about avoiding the existing one. We are not dealing here with this subject, because it does not matter. We leave it to those people interested in Law, Sociology or Philosophy. We bring it into consideration here for the reader would take it into account in case he ignored it. It is not the same to work as state agent in a European country or in a South American or African one.

And it is not because some countries are better or worse than others, but they are "different". Business is done differently. We try to know the previous requirements in our country to do the job of state agent. We have already said that it is not necessary to have a university degree, unless in most country of the world, as long as we know. That is settled. It is not the same as regards the previous requirements of the activity that depends of the place on earth where we are.

This book is an attempt to show that anyone can work as a state agent independently of the country where the reader is. As there are so many different cases from one society to another, we have to establish some generic patterns to be useful to everyone.

Each one will have to investigate in its own country the previous legal requirements to start this activity.

What do we have to do to start this activity if we are in Spain?

It is very simple.

In the beginning, we will have to follow two very important steps:

1. -Charge ourselves in the self employed registry in the social security, and

2. - Charge us in the Treasury Ministry

Legally speaking, this is the basic and fundamental requirements. Then you must ask permission in the Town Hall and enroll the activity in the Chamber of Commerce nearer to the place where you are going to open your office.

There are certain advantages related to this way of working as a stare agent.

Firstly it is the fact that to work on your own, without partners. Nothing can be more comforting than to be your own boss, you do not have to give explanations of every action you do, or any step you make.

Secondly it is the complication that implies the creation of an enterprise, as we will see in the next chapter. There are even more obstacles and troubles to solve in this sector if you want to work as a juridical person rather than a natural person. You have to create a name and you must contribute some essential minimum amount of capital, you have also to determine the type of enterprise, to register it according to the form of taxing, the employees it will have and their social security quotation, etc.

On the other hand, it is the fact that as a natural person we can stop the activity whenever we want without any complications. It is not the same with a person different to ourselves to whom we are administrating, and as a consequence, the steps to give in order to close activities will be many and very different.

But they are not all advantages. This job as a natural person brings consequences that we have to consider carefully before we decide for the best option. Maybe, the most important of all would be the obligations. When we work on our own, like in every act in our ordinary life, every step we take leaves us obliged to others. We are obliged to meet personally everything we have agreed. When we work through an interposed enterprise, the enterprise is the one bound to meet the contracted obligations by its administrative or managerial that represents it.

We must remember that it is a different person from ourselves, and consequently, it is capable of being holder of rights and obligations. This is the essence of the concept "person" from the legal point of view; it is anyone capable of being holder of rights and obligations.

The transcendence of this goes beyond the knowledge of who is obliged or not. When you acquire a legal obligation, you are responsible at a creditor. And here comes precisely the most important matter to consider: How do we answer?

There is a universal principle in Law that settles that the debtors are bound to pay with his own property goods "had" or "nearly to have". Whether it is a natural or juridical person, the responsibility of acts it is always patrimonial. There is no prison for debt, as it is usually said.

But here it is a substantial difference. The enterprises answer with their own patrimony. We answer with ours. If the enterprise cannot answer, files for bankruptcy. If we cannot answer, we would be indebted for the rest of our lives. If we cannot pay as long as we live, when we die, our obligations will be part of our inheritance, they will live out our own physical death. It will depend on our heirs whether they accept it or not, because when an inheritance is accepted we must get in charge of the good and the bad, that is to say, of the causative rights and obligations.

But in order to avoid going further in the speculation of possibilities, the most important is to state clearly the concept of "responsibility". When working as a real estate agent and obligations turn up. If The Real Estate Agent is a natural person, he will answer with his own patrimony, present or future, while if it is a "juridical persona", this administration will run with the obligations. They will answer with its patrimony, not with ours.

There are certain people, due to the reason we have explained before, that create an enterprise; and they do not risk his own patrimony in his commercial activities. It is not about the fact of being simple or "smart", but only cautious. If things do not go well, it is better to have some prevention.

When we start any type of activity or business, it is as important how to start it as how to go out of it. There is a popular saying in Spain that says: "To the best hunter escapes the hare". You can have the best intention of the world, the best of good will, and it happens that after all we realize, by any purpose, things are not going well in the activity. Being prevented is a wise thing.

But one thing is being conscious, and another is to pretend to be the smartest person in the world. It usually happens with the scammers and cheaters, they believe that the knowledge of how to cheat, allows them to get out unharmed. The following explanation is for them:

I do not mean that by the fact of creating an Enterprise for obliging it in case it was necessary and not us personally, to be extent of responsibility. The bad administration of an enterprise is causative of patrimonial responsibility on the part of its partner or people that act in their behalf. Here you cannot say: "It is not my responsibility but the enterprise". If it is possible to demonstrate bad intention, there would be patrimonial responsibility, even penal or criminal.

Commit crimes against current legality interposing an Enterprise, is a aggravated crime by fraudulent scratching in committing it.

That is why what we have said before it is only valuable to those that demonstrate that besides doing everything necessary for things to turn out well, due to unexpected causes we reach to an extend that the enterprise has no capacity to comply its obligations.

Fraudulent bankruptcy of an enterprise is a crime. It is also important to remember this.

CHAPTER 4

THE REAL ESTATE AGENT AS A JURIDICAL PERSON

The second way of work in the real estate business is by means of a juridical person, that is to say: an enterprise.

The concept of person, from the legal point of view, refers to individuals of human species as a well as other type of forms susceptible of being holders of rights and obligations. We have widely commented in the previous chapter.

There is a variety of subjects whom the law considers "juridical persons". For example, foundations, civil and/or trading associations, communities, states, etc. In this book we are interested in enterprise, the so called trading societies.

To start an Enterprise is a new subject. It is like to have a baby. We create this subject that is going to "live on its own". It is going to have definitely different life to its founders.

It has legal capacity to have debts, and assumes obligations. It also holds a series of rights upon its own goods. A person, either natural or juridical is not conceived without a patrimony. Patrimony is a set of rights and obligations susceptible of economical appreciation of which it is holder.

The enterprises are "abstractions" of the human mind converted into a person. They are "entities" which the law recognizes independent life of its own.

An advantage of working The Real Estate Agent as an enterprise, is that our possible customers will trust us more, unless as first impression. It is not the same a person who works on his own state agency, that an enterprise with its commercial place, its office to attend customers, with secretaries, its name and logo, advertising slogan, etc. They are two very different things.

Let's think of us: Who do we trust more? As we have also seen in the previous chapter, it is the question of responsibility. It is not the same a juridical person dealing business with the risk of its own patrimony at the possible obligations that would arise, than a person who faces the same situation with his personal and/or familiar patrimony.

Well, let's suppose that we have decided to create an Enterprise. What do we have to do? Which are the steps to follow? Let's consider them one by one.

1) COMMERCIAL NAME AND SLOGAN.

First of all we have to think of a name. How is it to be called?

In our case it should be an attractive name from the commercial point of view that denotes de activity we are going to carry on. It is only a suggestion for advertising purpose. Everyone can choose the name he wants. But it is not the same "Justino Real State" than "Justino and Company". In the first case, not the second, it comes to our mind the kind of business it is about.

Besides the name, we can also choose a representative image, a symbol or a slogan. Here comes into account the creativity of the founders. Let's see some examples.

An example of image would be a mushroom or a bush with a shape of a house.

An example of sign is the dollar or other coin sign.

Lastly, an example of slogan would be: "Our purpose is your wellness".

2) THE SELECTION OF ENTREPRICE TYPE

According the country we live in, we will inquire to a business agent or directly at the trading registry of our city, which are the basic constitution requirements.

We have to create an organization for profit. It is very important to have this in mind. We should not create a civil society or a foundation, because it is supposed they are entities that they do not pursue benefits, but other purposes (charity, philanthropic, etc.)

The two better known forms of associations for profit are Limited Liability Company (L.L.C.) and the Anonymous Society (A.S.), they are also called "Anonymous Companies" in certain countries.

The differences between them are that in the first ones the partners put a fee of participation, while in the second ones the holders put some of money as a share that can be sold or transferred to other people. The majority holder controls the enterprise and names the management positions. This is the commonly chosen type.

3) THE CONSTITUTIVE DOCUMENT

The constitutive document is the act of birth of our enterprise. We have to write on it, all the clauses inherent to its operation; the name and the slogan, the complete identification data of the partners, the contributed money (specified in cash, or in movable or immovable properties),the society address, the name of the managers or administrative staff, etc., etc., etc.

There is this type of documents in forms. We only have to fill in with the information and present them at the trade registry in the place where our enterprise is located. We do not have to complicate with this stage. We only comment it here as illustration.

Once the Enterprise document is registered, we have to go to the Treasure of Social

Security (in Spain) to register the employees who are going to work effectively. In the Spanish case, the partners have to register in the Autonomous Regime and not in the general one because it is not admitted by the law. The law only admits to register in the General Regime those employees or administrative clerks that are not partners.

We have also to take our document to the nearer Tributary Agency of our town for the correspondent tributary purposes.

At the end of this chapter there are two simple models of constitutive documents of enterprise attached as illustrative matters. The first is an example of Anonymous Socicty (A.S.) and the second is about the Limited Liability Society (L.L.S.).

4) COMMERCIAL HEADQUARTERS

This is the most important part. A good place is an image for confidence for customers. It is not the same if the enterprise is located in a busy avenue or in a path of a hidden commercial store.

We do not need much to start business in the headquarters of our enterprise. If we have a good amount of capital the better, but we do not have to worry if it is not too much if it is limited. The most important thing in this business is the human activity, not the headquarters.

What do we need basically?

1) Desks,

2) Chairs.

3) Telephone line

4) Internet connection

These are the basic things. Everything else we can add is good if it contributes to achieve of our purposes, but it is not essential.

We have already got our headquarters, with or without Enterprise. So let's go on.

ANNEXE

ANNEXE I

MODEL OF ANNONYMOUS SOCIETY

CONSTITUTIVE DOCUMENT

Title I. - DENOMINATION, DURATION, ADDRESS AND OBJECT

Article 1º. - Denomination.

The denomination of the society is "......................, A.S." and it will be ruled by the present statutes, as well as by de legal dispositions that are applied in every moment.

Article 2º. - Duration

The society will last indefinitely, starting business the day it will be provided by the written constitution, without any damage of the provided legal consequences for the acts and contracts celebrated in the name of the society in the previous moments of its registration in the Trade Registry.

Article 3º.- Social address

The effective social address and administration will be in………………………office number……………………………....on the………………………….floor at number………………………………………,……………..Street/Avenue/Road.

The administration organ can decide the creation, suppression and translation of branch offices.

Article 4º. - Social Object.

The society will have as social object…………………..

The listed activities can be developed by the Society direct or indirectly, total or partially, through the holding of shares or participating in societies with analogous or identical object.

TITLE II. - CAPITAL AND SHARES

Article 5º - Capital

The amount of capital is of Euros................................. (Minimum 60.000), y it is totally subscribed and disbursed. With general character and unless it is accorded the increase of capital and emission of new shares, the Council of Administration is empowered to establish the way and the dates in which the disburses will be timely made, when there are liabilities dividends and they have to be satisfied in metal, respecting the maximum time limit of 5 years.

When the pending liabilities dividends are to be disbursed by no money amounts, the General Meeting, that have accorded the increase of capital should determine the nature, value and content of the future contributions, besides the way and the process to make them and establishing the period of time, which never should exceed 5 years, since the date of the adoption of the corresponding agreement of increase of capital.

Article 6º- Number and representation of shares.

The capital described in Article 5º of these statutes are divided into……………………………….. nominative shares of Euros…………………………….nominal value each of them, being all of them the same type, and they are represented by nominative titles correlatively numbered from………………………….. to……………………………, both inclusive, they have the mentions required by Law.

All of them are subscribed and disbursed totally.

The society will/ will not be able to release provisional guards and multiple titles (it will depend on the conditions and requirements demanded by law)

Article 7º - Sharcholders Rights

Every share confers to its legitimate owner the condition of partner, to whom all the recognized rights will be attributed by Law in the present statutes

At least, every shareholder has the following rights:

* Right to participate in the distribution of social profits and in the patrimony resulted from the paying, in case this paying are the proper ones.

* Right of subscribing preferably in the releasing of new shares or, of obligations convertible in shares.

* Right to be informed.

* Right to decide and vote in the General Meetings of Society, and to oppose to social agreements. It is established the attribution of the right of a vote per share, thus the society reserves the right of emitting shares without vote in the quantity and with the legally established requirements.

Article 8°. - Transmition of shares Regime

The shares are appointment values freely transmittable according to Law

TITLE III. - SOCIAL ORGANS

Article 9°.-General dispositions.

They are organs in the society the General Meeting of Shareholders, as the supreme organ that manifests deliberately the social will for the most of matters of its interest, and the Council of Administration, to which it will belong the management functions, administration and representation of society, with the faculties that it has legally attributed, as well as those ones they are recognized in the present status.

First Section: General Meetings

Article 10º. - General Meeting

The shareholders that constitute valid and legally into General Meeting will decide in majority about matters that are competent to the Meeting.

All the shareholders, including the dissidents and the ones that have not participated in the meeting, are subjected to the agreements adopted by the General Meeting, without prejudice of its own impugnation right, in the legally provided suppositions, and when the precise requirements compete at such effect.

Article 11º. - Types of General Meetings

The General Meetings of the Shareholders could be ordinary and extraordinary, and they will be called by the social administrators.

The Ordinary General Meeting, that it will have been previously called, it will be celebrated in the necessary way within the six first months in every economical exercise with the object of censoring the social management, to approve, in its case the accountings of the previous exercise, and to solve about the application of the obtained result, according to the balance to be approved, without prejudice of other matters that can be treated in it, according to the prevailed in the Agenda.

All the different General Meetings from the ordinary General Meeting will be considered Extra-ordinaries General Meetings and they will be celebrated every time they are convenient or opportunely considered to the interests of the society and, in any case, when it is required by a number of shareholders of the at least 5% of the social capital, who will express in their application the affairs they consider they should deal in such Meeting. In this case, the meeting will be requested by the administrators to be celebrated in two months following the date required, and it should be included in the Agenda, at least, the affairs the Shareholders demanded by a formal written request.

Article 12º. - Place and date of celebration.

The General Meetings are celebrated in the location of the social address and in the dates established in the requirements, and it will prolong its sessions one or more consecutive days.

Universal Meetings will be celebrated in any place and town.

Article 13º. - Calling

The Ordinary General Meetings as well as the Extraordinaire will be called, previous agreement with the Administration Council, by its President, with an announcement published in the Official Bulletin of the Trading Registry and in the most selling newspaper of the state where the society is located. The announcement should be published with a month of anticipation.

In the published announce should be stipulated the date of the meeting in the second calling. In any case, there must mediate a minimum interval of 24 hours between the first and second calling.

If the second calling would not be prevented in the announcement of the first one, it must be called in the following fifteen days after the date of the cancelled one, with the same requirements of advertising, and with a term of eight days of anticipation, minimum, of the celebrating date.

In the calling of the Ordinary General Meeting it will be mandatory the expressed mention of the right of every shareholder to obtain the documents to be the object of approval freely and immediately.

In case the Ordinary or Extraordinary General Meeting decides any modifications in the present statutes, should be clearly expressed in the announcement of the calling, the extremes that pretend to modify and the law that assists to all the shareholders to examine at the social address the whole text of the proposed modifications and their reports to elaborate in the prescriptive way; in the same way they ask the delivery of these documents.

Besides what is settled in the previous paragraphs, it is possible the celebration of the Extraordinary or Ordinary General Meeting to deal any matters, without the presence of all the capital disbursed, the assistants are to accept by unanimity its celebration, so this meeting should be called Universal Meeting due to its characteristics.

The judicial Convocation will be ruled by the legal dispositions provided to such effect.

Article 14º. - Quorum in general assumptions.

Generally, the General Meeting, whether Ordinary or Extraordinary, will be constituted validly in the first calling when the shareholders present or represented will have at least 25% of the capital subscribed with the right to vote. (It can be established a superior quorum)

In the second calling it will be valid the celebration of a Meeting independently of its capital. /

Article 15º. – Quorum Specialties in determined assumptions.

However the preventions stated in the previous article, for the Extraordinary or Ordinary General Meeting to agree in reference of the emission of obligations, the increase or decrease of capital, the transformation, fusion, scission or dissolution of the society because any of the causes provided in article 363 in the text of the Law of Society of Capital, and in general, to valid the adoption of any type of agreement that imply any modification of any of the present statutes. In this case it is necessary to celebrate the Meeting, in the first calling, and with the representation of at least 50% of the subscribed capital with right to vote.

In the second calling it will be necessary the presence of shareholders or representatives that have got at least 25% of the capital subscribed with right to vote. But if the shareholders present in the meeting represent less than 50% of the capital, the mentioned agreements can only be validated with positive vote of two third parts of the capital present or represented in the Meeting. (It can be fixed quorum or higher majorities).

Article 16º. - Attendance to the Meetings

Any shareholder that has his shares inscribed in the Book Register of Nominative Shares, with at least 5 days of anticipation of the date of celebration of the meeting, can participate personally or on behalf of other person, independently of the character of the shareholder.

For purposes of attendance on behalf of a representation of the shareholders they will have the right to ask and obtain the correspondent card of assistance from the society, in any moment since the publication of the calling till the beginning of the Meeting.

The representation should be given in written by any distance means of communication that meet the requirements provided for the exercise of the right to vote in the distance contemplated in the following article, and with special character to each Meeting, except in cases in which the represented is the spouse, ascendant or descendant of the represented, or when it is given faculties to manage all the patrimony that the person represented has got in National territory.

The Administrators should also attend to General Meetings. Besides the Directors, Managers, Agents, Technicians and other people that the President of the Meeting considered they should be present in the meeting because they are interested in social matters. The President of the Meeting will authorize, in principle, the attendance of any other people that he considers convenient, and the Meeting can revoke such authorization.

Article 16º Bis. - Remote vote

The proposals about the issues in the agenda of any type of the General Meetings could be delegate or exercise by any shareholder by postal or electronic mailing or any other means of remote communication that certainly assure the identity of the person that exercise his right to vote. (It can be pointed out the identity guaranty mechanisms, for example: to ask for an affidavit for the vote sent by mail or to ask for a certified emission of it, or a digital signature in case it is emitted by electronic mail, etc.)

The shareholders that emit their votes remotely will be taken into account for the constitution of the meeting as present members.

Article 17º. - Constitution of the table.

The General Council President, or the vice-president in his absence, or in case both are absent, the Counselor or the elected shareholder by the majority of the shareholders present in the meeting, will head the General Meeting of Shareholders.

The Secretary:............................. of the Council will act as the Meeting Secretary, or in default, it will be substituted by the Assessor Lawyer of the Society in case he was a different person that the Secretary, or in both default, the Counselor or the Shareholder elected by the majority of the present shareholders in the meeting.

Before starting the debate of the listed matters in the agenda, the list of assistants with the previous legal requirements should be elaborated.

Article 18º. - Deliberations.

The President will guide the deliberations conceding the right to speak, rigorously, to every shareholder that asks for it in written note, and afterwards to those who ask for this right orally.

Article 19º. - Voting and Agreements subscription.

Each of the points included in the agenda should be voted separately. The agreements adopted by the majority of the present or represented shareholders, except the provided cases in Article 15 of the present statutes, regarding the second calling to the meeting in which the present capital is less than the 25% of the subscribed capital with right to vote, postulation in which it is needed the majority of both thirds of the present or represented capital in the Meeting. Each share gives right to a vote.

Article 20º. - The Acts of the Meetings

The deliberations and agreements of the General Meetings, both ordinary and extraordinary should be written in the proper Book of Acts, and they should be signed by the entitled President and Secretary, or by the ones that have acted in the stated meeting on their behalf.

The act could be approved by the Meeting at the end of its celebration, or in default, within a term of 15 days, subscribed by the President and two controllers, one of them named by the majority and the other by the minority.

The Managers under their own initiative, when they decided it or when it is compulsory reliably asked in written in terms of five days in advanced from the celebration of the Meeting in the first shareholders calling that represent at least one percent of the social capital, will require the present of a Notary to write an act of the Meeting, and the honorarium of the elected Notary should be paid by the society. The notary act will be considered the act of the Meeting.

Article 21º. - Certifications.

The Secretary or, in default, the Vice-secretary of the Administration Council, has the faculty to certificate the Acts and the General Meeting Agreements.

The certifications will be emitted with the supervision of the President of the Council, or in default, of Vice-President.

Article 22º. - Execution of Agreements

The only people empowered to execute the social agreements and to give the correspondent public documents are those authorized to certificate the social agreements according the previous article, besides the members of the Administration Council whose inscription was actual and registered in the Trading Registry, and the people empowered by the Administration Organ.

Second Section. - Council of Administration.

Article 23º. - General Disposition.

The society will be arranged, managed and represented in the trial of outside it in every act included in the social object by a Council of Administration constituted by a number of…………………….. As minimum (three or more) ……………………….. As maximum (it can be settle a fixed number), that act collegially, notwithstanding of delegations and empowerment that can confer.

The determination of the number of Counselors, their designation and separation in any moment is competence of the Meeting, although it is not in the current agenda. The Council can only name as administrator a shareholder in a vacant place. It will be covered till the following meeting of the Ordinary or Extraordinary General Meeting after this naming. The Council will mane, among its members, a President, a Vice-president and………………………vocal members.

Article 24º. - Duration of charges.

The Counselors will be named by an equal term for all of them of………………………… and they could be reelected by the Meeting once or more times for periods of equal maximum lasting.

The naming will be understood extended till the first General Meeting to be celebrated after its expiration or till the provided time has expired for the Ordinary General Meeting.

Article 25º. - Presidency of the Council

The President of the Council is also the President of the Society and besides the inherent faculties of the rest of the Counselors he will add the following ones:

1º. - To head, direct, open and close the sessions of the Administration Council and the General Meetings of the Shareholders, as well as to decide the callings and to act in conformity when it is necessary, signing the announcements and correspondent publications.

2º. - Sign the title or validation of the shares or other obligations emitted by the Society.

3º. - Watch over the proper operation of the Society, trying and demanding the strict compliment of the agreements adopted by the Administration and by the General Meeting of Shareholders.

4º. - Watch over the Books of Acts of the General Meetings of the Society and the Administration Council, as well as the Registry Book of Nominative Shares, authorizing by the signature of successive transmissions that will occur.

5º. - Authorize by the signature the acts of the meetings of the General Meetings of Shareholders and the Administration Council.

In case of absence or illness of the President or the vacancy of this charge, it will substitute the Vice president, and in his absence the Vocal............................. .

Article 26º. - Calling of the Administration Council Meetings.

The Council will meet when it is required by the interest of the society, and when it is necessary within the first three months of each exercise, to approve the annual accountings of the previous exercise and the report of the management, as well as in every other case in which the General Meeting of Shareholders should be called.

The Council will be called by its President or the person on his behalf.

The calling will be written, and sent with.................... days in advance, except in the postulations in which it will be called in urgency according to the circumstances.

The President will call the Meeting when he considers it pertinently for the social interest, and in every case, by a request of..............................chancellors.

It will be considered validly constituted when half plus one of its members are present or represented. Any chancellor can grant his representation to other chancellor, in written form and with the expressed character for the meeting in question.

Article 27°. - Quorum and adoption of agreements of the Administration Council.

To adopt the agreements of the Council it will be necessary the positive vote of the absolute majority of the counselors present in the session, except in the case of permanent delegation of any faculty of the Administration Council in the Executive Commission or in the Delegated Counselor, and the designation of the managers that have to be in these charges, these matters will need positive vote of the two of the third parts in the members of the Council.

The voting will be done in writing and without session will be proceeding when none of the Counselors has opposed to this system.

The discussions and agreements of the Council will be transcribed in the Book of Acts, each of them to be signed by the President and the Secretary of the Council or by the person that has represented them in the meeting transcribed in the act.

In case of the voting in written and without session will be also transcribed in the Book of Acts of the adopted agreements and of the emitted written votes.

Article 28°. - Delegation of faculties and empowerments.

The Council could design an Executive Commission or one or more delegated Counselors, and delegate among them any or all the faculties legally delegable.

Both, the permanent delegations and such designation of the managers in charge of them will require the positive vote of the two thirds of the members of the Council to validate it.

However the Council could give powers to the whole class, and it can equally proceed to the naming of a General Director.

Article 29º. - Faculties of the Council.

The Administration Council will have the wider faculties to administrate, manage, and represent the society in trials, and outside them and in every act included in the social mean that is defined in Article 4º of the present social statutes.

The Administration Council will oblige the Society against third parties that have contracted in good faith and without serious fault, even when the act it is not included in this social object.

In merely enunciatively character, it is expressly recognized in the following faculties of the Council.

1st. - To design among its members a President and a Vice President. It can also design a Secretary that it is not required to be member of the Council.

2nd.- To agree the calling of the extraordinary and ordinary Meetings in the mode and moment in which they proceed, according to the legal requirements and the ones stated in the present statutes, written in the correspondent Agenda and make any proposals they considered convenient, according to the nature of the called Meeting.

3rd.- To represent the society in every matter and administrative and judicial acts, at the State Administration and public corporations of any order, any instance making any kind of actions corresponding to the defense of its rights, in judgments and outside them, empowering the attorneys to name lawyers to represent and defend the society at the mentioned courts and organisms.

4th. - To direct and administer the social business, attending the management of them constantly, according to the government rules, and the management regime and the operation of the society and organizing and regulating the technical and administrative services.

5th.- Celebrate any kind of contracts about any type of goods or rights, by means of agreements or conditions that consider convenient, and to constitute and cancel mortgages and other liens or real rights upon the goods of the society, this like to quit, paying or not, any type of privileges or rights. It could equally decide upon the participation of the society in other enterprises or societies.

6th.- To sign and acting in name of the society in every class of banking operations, opening and closing current account, disposing of them, intervening in Bills of exchange, promissory notes and other titles like, drawer, acceptor, guarantor, endorser, or holder of them, to ask for credits, with or without guaranty, and cancel them, to make transferences of money, rents, credits or values, by any procedure of transferences or money movements, approve balances of closed accounts, constitute or withdraw deposits or bails, compensate accounts, to formalize changes, etc, with the Bank of Spain and Official Bank and with private banks or any other organization of the Administration of the State or of any other autonomous communities or local organizations.

7th.- To name, destine, dismiss, make every necessary actuation with reference to the staff working in the society, to assign salaries, gratifications, compensations, etc. when proceeding and to fix general expenses of administration.

8th. - To name and design, and to separate agents, concessionaire, commission agents, and correspondents that have the Society.

9th.- To carry on and withdraw the administrations of Mailing and telegraphers, letters, certificates, postal orders, declared values, telegrams, and telegraphic orders, open the mailing and answer them.

10th. - To contract any type of insurance.

11th.- To intervene in the interruption of payment, bankruptcy, removals and waiting; to name administrative receivers, to accept or refuse the proposals of agreement with debts, the accounts of administrators and the graduation of the credits, to admit in payment or to pay debts, assignment of goods of any class from any debt.

12th. - Ask permission for the new implantation, reform, or widen, or modifications of industries or business.

13th.-To designate among its members an Executive Commission or one or more Delegate Counselors to delegate in them the conformity with the legal previsions, any faculties considered convenient, indicating in any case in the agreement of designation the regime of acting to follow in his relations with the Council and with the members of the Executive Commission or with the Delegated Counselors to be designed. It can also grant powers to any person.

14th. To regulate its own working in every aspect that is not legally included previously or in the present statutes, keeping safe every case all the faculties corresponding to the General Meeting of Shareholders.

15th. - To formalize and subscribe the private or public documents to be precisely effective in faculties.

Article 30º.-Payment

The retribution of the managers will be of ……………………………………………

TITLE IV. - SOCIAL EXCERCISE AND ANNUAL ACCOUNTS

Article 31º.- Social Exercise

The social exercises will start on 1st of January and will finish on 31st. of December of every year.

Article 32º. - Annual Accounts

In the maximum term of three months since the close of every economical exercise the Council should formulate the Annual Accounts, including in them the Balance, the Profit and Loss accounts and the Explicative Memory, the report of management and the proposal of applications of the results, according to the valuation criteria and with the legal structure, and demanded by regulation, and in this case, it should write the accounts and the report of management consolidated, that should sign all the administrators, expressing in default the missing signature of any cause.

Article 33º. - The deposit and advertising of the Annual Accounts. When the Annual Accounts are approved by the General Meeting they will be presented for their deposit, with the certification of the Agreement of the Meeting, in the corresponding Trading Registry, in the regulated term and legal forms.

Article 34º. - Application of the result.

The application of the result of the exercise is competence of the General Meeting, with the legal and statutory limits.

The dividends will be distributed among the ordinary shareholders in proportion to the capital invested.

TITLE V. - DISOLUTION AND SETTLEMENT OF THE SOCIETY

Article 35º. - Dissolution

The society will be dissolved in the cases and with the requirements established by law.

Article 36º. - Settlement Types

The General Meeting that agrees the dissolution of the society will equally name the liquidators that could be the same members of the Council of Administration.

The number of liquidators will always be an odd number, and in the cases it is decided the counselors make this function and the number of Counselors has been an even number, it will decided however that the vocal member will not be designated as liquidator or that other person will make with the counselors then liquidator, such liquidator functions, as it is agreed.

Article 37º.-Settlements Standards.

In the liquidation of the society the standards established by law will be watched, and the complementary to these respecting the legal meetings, they were agreed by the General Meeting of Shareholders that has adopted the agreement of the dissolution.

TITLE VI.- SUPLEMENTARY REGIMEN

Article 38º. - Supplementary Regimen

In everything that is not provided in the previous articles of the present statutes It will apply the regulations of the Law of Anonymous

Societies, from the Trading Code and the Regulations of the Trading Registry.

ANNEXE II

MODEL OF CONSTITUTIVE DOCUMENT OF A SOCIETY OF LIABILITY LIMITED (L.L.S)

TITLE I. - DENOMINATION, DURATION, ADDRESS AND OBJECT

Artículo 1º.-Denomination

The Society will be denominated ".. .... Society of Liability Limited" and it will be ruled by its constitutive contract, by the present statutes and in the things that are not included, by the Law of Society of Capital.

Article 2º. - Duration

The Society will have a duration of indefinite character, beginning with the starting its operations the following day after receiving the constitutive deed, notwithstanding of the legal consequences provided for the acts and contracts in name of the Society in previous moments to the inscription in the Trading Registry.

The social exercises are computed by natural years.

Article 3º. - Address

The Society is located in………………………….nº…………,……………
…………….street, Office……………………..

Article 4º.- Social Object

The social object of the Society will be………………………..

TITLE II. - SOCIAL CAPITAL AND PARTICIPANTS

Article 5º. - Social Capital

The social capital will be of €uros..., divided into...............................participation of €uros..............................., of nominal value each of them, correlative numbered from 1 to ....

This capital is totally subscribed and disbursed in contributions (money/no money) made by founder partners as property title.

Article 6º. - Prohibitions about participations

The participations cannot be incorporated to Securities; neither represented by means of annotations in count, nor be named shares.

Article 7º. - Title of property on the participations.

It cannot be emitted accredited provisional reservations of the property upon one or more social participations, being the constitutive deed the only property title of the Society or, in case, the public documents in which the subsequent acquisitions of such participations are credited.

Article 8°. - Registry Book of Partners

The society will run a Registry Book of partners whose custody and writing is responsibility of the Administration organ, in which it will record the original entitlement and the successive transmissions, voluntary or forced, of the social participations, and the constitution of the real rights and other liens that can be made upon them, indicating in each annotations the identity and address of the title of the participations or of the right of constituted lien upon them.

It can only be rectified its content if the interested people do not agree to do it in the term of a month from the reliable notifications of its procedure purpose.

Any partner will have the right to examine the content of the Book, and he will also have the right to obtain certifications of the participations, rights or liens registered in its name both partners and entitled people of the real rights and or liens that can appear in it.

The personal data of the partners could be modified in its instance, without working in the meantime upon the society.

Article 9°. - General rules about transmissions of the participations and constitution of the charges or liens upon them.

Every transmission of the social participations or constitution of charges or liens upon them should be in public document, and they should be communicated in written to the Society.

Article 10°. - Transmissions

A) Voluntary by inter live acts.

It will be free every voluntary transmission of social participations made by inter live acts, onerous or free, among partners, as well as the transmissions made in favor to the spouse, ascendant or descendants of the partner, or in favor of societies belonging to the same group of the transmitting one, in terms established in the Trading Code, Article 42.

The other transmissions by inter live acts will be subjected to that settled by law.

B) Mortis cause.

It will be free every mortis cause transmission of the social participations, by inheritance or legated in favor of other partner, in favor of the spouse, ascendant or descendant of the partner.

Out of these cases, in the other mortis cause transmissions of the social participations the survivor partners, and in default the Society, will have a right of acquisition, preferable of the social participations that belongs to the deceased, appreciated in the reasonable value that had at the date on which the partner has passed away, and whose price will be paid on cash; this right should be practiced in the maximum term of three months from the communication of the inherited acquisition to the Society.

In absence of agreement about the reasonable value of the social participations or about the person or people that have to value them and the procedure to follow to that act of value, the participations will be valued in terms provided in the article 100 and the followings in the Law of Liability Limited Societies.

Once the term is due in time, and it has not truly exercised this right, it will be consolidated the inherited acquisition.

C) Common Rules.

1.- The acquisition, by any title, of social participations, should be communicated in written to the administration organ of the Society, indicating name or social denomination, nationality and address of the acquirer.

2. The regimen of the transmission of the social participations will be valid the date in which the partner had communicated to the society the purpose to transmit or, in this case, the date in which the partner has passed away, or the date of the judicial or administrative adjudication.

3. The transmission of social participations that are not subjected to the provided in these statutes will not produce any effect upon de society.

Article 11º. - Co-propriety, usufruct, pledge and mortgage of the social participations

The co-propriety, usufruct, pledge and mortgage of the social participations will be ruled by the legal dispositions provided to that effect.

TITLE III. SOCIAL ORGANS

Article 12°. - General Meeting.

A) Calling

The general meetings will be called by individual written announcement that will be sent by postal mail with the acknowledgement of receipt to the address indicated in the Book of Partners Registry.

The partners living in foreign countries should designate an address in the national territory to receive notifications.

B) Adoption of agreements

The social agreements will be adopted by the majority of the valid emitted votes, every time they represent at least a third of the corresponding votes of the social participations in which the social capital is divided, without computing the blank votes.

a) From more than a half of the votes corresponding to the participations in which the social capital is divided, for the agreements about the increasing or reduction of the social capital, or any other modification of the social statutes for the qualified majority is not required that it is indicated in the following apart.

b) From at least two thirds votes corresponding to the participations in which the social capital is divided, for the referent agreements, or the transformation, fusion or excision of the society, to the suppression of the right of preference in the increasing of the capital, to the exclusion of partners, to the authorization of the administrators to dedicate in representation of others or on his own, to the same, analogous or complementary genre of activity that constitute the social object.

The above mentioned is understood without prejudice of the preferable application of the legal imperative dispositions that, to specific agreements, will ask the consentient of all the partners or impose specific requirements.

Article 13º. - Administration Organ: organization.

1. The administration of the society can be trusted to a one-person organ (only administrator), to many solidarity administrators, to many joint administrators or to a council of administration with a minimum number of …… administrators and a maximum of ……. administrators.

2. The general meeting, with its qualified majority and without implied statutory modification, has the faculty to choose any mode to organize the administrations of the Society.

3. The administrators will exercise their charges by an indefinite time, except that he General Meeting, after the constitution, determines its nomination by a determined term.

4. The administrator charge is not remunerated.

Article 14º. - Power of representation.

Regarding the different types of administration organs, it is settle the followings:

1. In case there is an only Administrator, the power of representation is upon itself.

2. In case there are many solidarity Administrators, the power of representation will be on all of them.

3. In case there are many joint Administrations, the power of representations will be exercised jointly by any two of them.

4. Whenever it is about a Council of Administration, it will work collegially.

Article 15º. - Regime of Council of Administration

1. Composition

The Council of Administration will choose a President and a Secretary out of its members, one or many Vice presidents or Vice secretaries, in case such nominations were not done by the General Meeting or the founders at the time of designing the Counselors.

2. Calling

The calling of the Council is the President's duty, or who represents him, who has this faculty, whenever they consider it convenient and in any case, when it is called by at least two counselors, in such case it will be called to be celebrated within the fortnight following the call.

The calling will be made by personal written note to each Counselor and sent to their address designed for this purpose by them, or on lack of special determination, to the registry one, five days before the date of the meeting; it will also include, day, time and place of the meeting. Except unanimous agreement, the place of the meeting will be fixed in the town council corresponding to the address of the society.

The Council will be validly constituted, without previous calling, every time they are present all of its members, and all of them accept by unanimity its celebration.

3. Representation.

Every Council could have been represented by other. The representation will be given in written and with special character for every meeting, by means of a letter sent to the President.

4. Constitution

The Council will be validly constituted when they go to the meeting, present or represented, more than a half of its members.

5. Deliberations and Agreements

All the Counselors will have the right to manifest about every matter to consider, without prejudice is the President duty to grant the right to speak and the duration of the interventions.

Necessarily will submit to vote the proposals of agreements presented by, at least, two Counselors. Each member of the Council can emit one vote. The agreements will adopt the absolute majority of the coming Counselors to the session, except the specific legal disposition.

The vote of the President will be diriment.

6. Act

The discussions and agreements of the Councils will have a book of acts that will be signed by the President and the Secretary, within a period of seven days since the celebration of the meeting of the Council, if they were authorized by unanimity the Counselors assisting to it.

7. Delegation of faculties

The Administration Council can designate an Executive Commission within or one or many Delegate Counselors, determining in any case, the particular enumeration of the faculties that are delegated, good expression is that they are "delegated" all the legal statutorily delegable faculties.

The delegation can be temporal or permanent. The permanent delegation and the designation of its titular will require the favorable vote of at least two third parts of the members of the Council and will not produce any effect till its inscription in the Trading Registry.

8. Auto-regulation

In the unforeseen things, and if nobody opposes to the imperative dispositions, the Council could regulate its operations.

TITLE IV. - SOCIAL EXCERCISE AND ANNUAL ACCOUNTS

Article 16º. - Social Exercise

The social exercises start on 1st January and finish on 31st December every ordinary year.

As exception, the first social exercise includes since the beginning of the operations of the Society till the 31st December of the same year.

Article 17º. - Annual Accounts

The accounts and the managing reports, as well as its revision by accounts auditors, should adjust to the actual legal regulatory dispositions in every minute.

The dividends distribution to the partners will be done in proportion to its participation in the capital.

The partners have the right to examine the accounting in the terms provided by Law.

TITLE V. - DISOLUTION AND SETTLEMENT OF THE SOCIETY

Article 18º. - Dissolution and settlement

1. The dissolution and liquidation of the society, in cases not provided by these Statutes, will be subjected to the special dispositions within the law.

2. The Administrators at the time of the dissolution will be converted into the liquidators except that, when agreeing the dissolution, they are designed by the General Meeting.

CHAPTER 5

THE SATE AGENT JOB, ATRIBUTIONS AND FUNCTIONS

We are going to analyze The Real Estate Agent function. This is something we must always keep in mind. The answers to the questions: What do we do? What is our job about?

Let's start now an analysis of the function of The Real Estate Agent. We have to take into account the answer to these questions: What do we do?, What is our job about?

Let's define it.

A State Agent is simply another seller. It is a person who sells something. This "something" is his human activity, his services.

When we talk about the seller, many people think it is a man with a case calling at the door to convince people to buy a device. Actually this way of selling represents less than 1% of the total of sales that are made on earth every day, including The Real Estate Agent business section.

Any seller, do not sale goods, but ideas. They sell the idea that we need the things they sell. They try to influence on our belief of how useful it will result, and how much do we need it.

Here are some examples.

Let's start with the stars; the religious. The Jehová Witnesses, for example, they sell their ideas of the endless life, the forgiveness of sins, the redemption of souls, etc. They try by all means, to influence upon us to "buy" them these beliefs. They do not sell an object, a good, like a vacuum cleaner, or an orange juice extractor, or an insurance policy. But they are sellers like many others.

The supermarket owners are also sellers. But they do not go from house to house visiting people trying to influence on their ideas. They use another type of strategies. They make advertising campaign, keep their shops clean and ordered, they try to compete with good prices, give good attention to clients training his workers to be kind and smiley, etc. But they are not less sellers than the Jehovah Witnesses or the vacuum cleaners sellers. They use other methods.

The owners of Banks are also sellers. The Banks sell their services, and you do not see their owners or shareholders calling at the doors, from house to house offering opening an account or offering loans or a credit card. They use other strategies.

The seducers and lovers are also sellers. They sell their image of smart people, or in default, of people with resources or that they have "something" that can interest to the seduced one.

In one way or another, all of us are sellers. Whether we work in any of the multiple ways of selling, simply because we use any technique or strategy to get what we want. Because, finally what we are actually doing is to sell our ideas. If they buy them, we get what we want: Our price.

The seller is a "seducer", although this word may sound a bit hard. The owner of a supermarket chain will try to seduce us with advertising to buy in their stores and not in others.

The human mind is like a camcorder that it is always on. It never stops. The brain works even when sleeping. It is like the heart. It never stops.

When I travel along an avenue and I see a supermarket advertising banner, this idea keeps in my mind to remember it involuntarily every moment. When I remember that I have to do the shopping, my brain will tell me that this supermarket is stored among my options. I will decide whether I go to this supermarket or to another. But the recording of the image and its message, implicit or explicit, was given, and it will never be erased.

As we can see, the sale is not more than a game of psychological strategies.

As any seller, a State Agent has to develop his own strategies and methodology to achieve his goals. And there are hundreds of them. In this text we will deal with some of them, the most useful. It will depend of the people to pick up his own way to meet the objectives.

There are not magical recipes. Every seller knows or has to make efforts to know his own limits, and the levels of their inner potentialities. It will depend on the personal characteristics.

In this book we will suggests some tips. Anyone is free to take them or leave them. We emphasize this because some critics we received in the first edition. They said they were against moral and ethics. May be they were true. This is not a book about moral, but business. And in the business world it is necessary to know the good and bad sides. You can choose.

We do not teach to break the law; on the contrary, we teach how to get profits within the law so you are happy.

Needless to say this book is not from moralist and pious people. Here we teach how to earn money, a lot of money, as a state agent. Is this job against moral? Maybe

We have to say in our legitimate defense that moral is always subjective; people consider some things good or bad. Everyone sees things his own way. The moral is a personal individual construction of values. If these techniques used in the underworld of immovable properties business do not admit consideration, The Real Estate Agent will always have some other options to choose. Here you will find all of them, starting with the most aggressive ones.

Maybe some of you consider indecent and immoral to travel round the world in a luxurious cruise, taking advantage of the benefits of a most worthy job, while so many people are in need in the world. Or maybe other people think it is not ethic to earn in a day an amount of money other people could earn working as slaves in many years.

All these are respectful opinions. Everyone is free to think and choose what to do with their lives. Let's go on.

We can deduce from we have said before that there are many strategies in the sale world. The strategy to use will depend on the product to sale. Different products require distinct strategies.

Some products sell themselves; they do not need a hardworking and kind seller. This is the case of human consume products. For example bread.

The hardworking seller has to keep clean and attractive his bakery, to choose a good location and to make a variety of good quality bread. If his variety and quality is better than his competitors' would be even better. It will be always useful to have a smart, kind and cordial and fast seller; these are additional to his sale strategies but not the principal. If the bread is not of a good quality although the seller is kind, people will buy bread at another bakery. If the place is dirty permanently and cause bad impression, clients would prefer to buy at another baker's. All the factors influence when aiming at the final objective: "to sell".

Another similar example would be a Variety Store owner, which sells multiple articles. In this case the owner efforts will be concentrated in having at hand the neediest articles for the consumers, the cleaning and order of the place, advertising, a good location and to compete with the prices and after sale service, and try to be kind and warm with clients for them to come back. But the clients are in charge of the elections of products, not the owner. Although the kindness of the seller is an important decisive factor, it is not the most important sale resource, but the sum of all of them.

In the case of the Immovable Management, the main sale resource is the Agent himself, but not the only one obviously. A good office, optimum location, some or a lot of advertising will sum up. But the essence of this business is in the seller himself; in The Real Estate Agent.

Although our office were very well located, clean and presentable, if we are not good at customer support, it will be very difficult to reach our goals. Although we do much advertising, if we are not capacitated enough to close business we are destined to fail.

Thus we have to polish ourselves; because we are our own resource and the essence in our job.

The Real Estate Agent must be a person with very particular virtues and qualities. The main of them, is the one of the "seducer". Yes, as you can see it: "seducer".

He will have to "seduce" his clients (in the good sense of the word). Once in love, the majority part of the job will be done. The rest will come out.

When we mention the Word "seduce", we refer to the capacity of influence on other people.

It is indispensable that the person who choose this job, will develop deeply the power to convince; the capacity of persuasion. This is the core of the matter. The axis around his world has to turn.

A person who is able to persuade, to convince other people, has the world at his feet.

He will not need a university degree, neither to make an effort to get a specific job. He will always get what he wants.

There are many examples.

Hundreds of people dedicate to give conferences talking about nuisance and they live on that. How do they do it? Making you believe in that what you hear have sense, have value. They are smoke sellers. People convince other people about kindness or profits of absurd products. Since miraculous "growing hair" potions till cancer cure treatments. There is everything. The most surprising fact is that all of them get astronomic earnings. They are people able to sell everything, because their capacity to influence on other people is so good that they get what they want.

Fortunately, it is not our case. We will not sell smoke, but a very concrete human activity, with tangible results.

As another seller The Real Estate Agent should direct his efforts to the development and perfection of the capacity of capt attract, convince. This is the essence of his job, and more than that, he should make of it his living.

It is not impossible. All of us can do it. For better or worse. This depends on our indispensable reinforcement of our personality, the rising of our esteem, and the belief that we can achieve everything we propose to do. This is a difficult aim to reach, if you think so, because our reality is very simple.

Whether you think something is possible or not, both cases are true. The thought belongs to Henry Ford, the founder of automobile enterprise "Ford Motor Company", one of the richest men of his time.

One of the most famous people in the world regarding love affairs was the Italian actor Rodolfo Valentino, famous for his unbelievable capacity of seducing, of attracting. It is said that many people committed suicide when he died at very early age; 31 years old. Some people throw out themselves wrapped into his photographs from high buildings.

In an interview he was made in one occasion, a journalist asked him what his secret was, and he answered without being upset that it was not in his physical beauty, of course. His secret was in the capacity of increasing the ego of the person to whom he was speaking. And how does he make it? They asked him again. His answer was also simple: "Speaking always about themselves."

When you always speak to someone about himself, exalting his virtues, he magically falls rendered at our feet. It is not an exaggeration. If it is faked we realize about it immediately. It would not be a sincere compliment the fact that a seller who calls at a house where an old centennial lady answers and he greets: "Good morning young lady. Is your mother at home?"-. This sounds as bullying.

We like to be flattered, be liked, and be well treated. It is not a question of simple preference. It is an innate need, intrinsic of the human being. Our personalities are defined by the more or less affective levels we may have received in our childhood. We always need affect. That is the reason we feel so good when we go to a restaurant and we are well attended.

Independently of the better or worse the food was, we will always remember the way we were treated, more than the flavor of food. If the treatment was kind and cordial, we would like to come back. It was despotic or unkind, we would not. The liking of the food can be resolved. We can always ask for another plate in a new occasion. But be bad treated will be recorded in our brains under the form of rejection, and when we consider options to dine out, this restaurant will be the first to discard.

This type of need is the one that any seller takes into account; the some sellers and the others.

FRANKLIN DÍAZ

CHAPTER 6

CUSTOMERS PORTFOLIO

Let's study the way of making customers now. This is one of the most important aspects in our job. It is our way of living in this activity.

It is always necessary to have in mind the object of our sale. Our offer is very clear and simple. We offer a well defined service; the intermediation. No more than that.

There are people who have the economical possibility of buying and selling immovable properties, or they buy and rent them, making of this business their living. This book was not thought for them.

This book is dedicated to those who want to dedicate to this activity as intermediaries, as agents. We have already said in our definition in the first chapter: "The Real Estate Agent is a person, natural or juridical, that in his own name or on other people behalf INTERMEDIATES between those who want to make juridical business with an immovable property."

This book is dedicated to the people who want to prepare themselves as intermediaries in the underworld of immovable properties business.

Let's go on.

It is not appropriate to include a kind of "miscellaneous" in our catalogue of functions. "Who wants to do a lot, the less he can achieve". It would not be very well seen that we included some matters which are not directly related to our activity.

I would not be proper that in our places, we also offer kindergarten services, or some bakery, etc. We clear this out because although it may sound crazy, there are people who actually do it.

Some people specialized in leasing, while others do the same with the sales. We will choose the better for us according to practice.

Remember that this text is dedicated to those who never worked in the underworld of real states business and pursue basic knowledge to start this activity.

CLIENTS TYPOLOGY

From the personality point of view, there is such variety of clients as ways of behaving of human beings, from the most difficult personalities to the less complicated ones. We will discuss later the way we should treat them. Now we will consider the type of clients from the point of view of the operations they pretend to do.

In this case, there are four kinds of clients:

1. - Sellers

2. - Lessors

3. - Purchasers

4. – Lessers

1. - SELLERS:

The only people who can be a seller are the ones capable to transmit the property right upon a good. Only the right holders can do it, on their own or by means of a leased operator.

This detail is especially relevant when it is about a common property. This is the case of inherited properties, community or society.

In all these cases it is indispensable that every co-owner agreed to sell. It is impossible to do it if there is only one of them against the idea. The rights upon an immovable property cannot be sold separately. It cannot also be sold in parts whether they belong to a society or a community. They are considered a generic part of a whole and it is not specific.

A co-owner of a house cannot sell by his own one of the rooms, or a yard, the garage, etc. Because, his rights, as well as the rest of the co-owners', are diluted in the whole propriety that it is not the addition of every concrete parts but the universality. Thus, if all the parts do not agree in selling, they have to present at the court to ask for the partition of the community or the society in question. Once it is resolved, the sale can be done. Not before.

In the previous chapter we commented we can bring out here. We said that the owner is the person who appears as such in the Immovable Property Registry. In this way, this types of immovable operations are safe and trustful for those contractors because the operations will be made directly in the Property Registry offices, in presence of a notary that certificate the identifications of the contract parts and they make the register afterwards. This is related to what will see now.

2. - LESSORS

It is necessary to have legal capacity in order to be a lessor. And we are not talking of being a grown up adult, or the case of not being legally entitled to dispose of their goods. This is a question that it is presumed as preexistence.

We refer to a capacity to dispose upon a good. Who is it attributed?

We are ready to answer this question.

As we know from the beginning, this capacity is attributed to the owner of the immovable property, as it is his right, it is implied the faculty to dispose his good as he wishes, without any other limits as the ones established by law. We have already discussed it in the previous chapters.

In this case is similar to the one of the sellers. There is no problem when there is only one owner entitled with the property right upon a good. He can offer his property for rent when he wants. But when there are many owners they have to make an agreement. It will be impossible if some of them are against the idea, because the transaction cannot be done.

It is not equal when selling. The renting contracts do not register. They can be certificate at the notary to reinforce a public document. To convert a private document, that only has effects on the contractors, into a public one and, as a consequence, to have effects upon third persons.

Notaries are public workers whose job consist of giving public faith of whom present upon him, are the people who say they are, and they also say what it is written in a document, without considering its veracity. These are his competences.

This is relative, because there are countries in which notaries have more attributions than the ones stated here. But it is not necessary to list all of them in this text, because it is not transcendental to the objectives we consider here, besides it is impossible to mention here the worldwide casuistry. We consider what happens in most of the countries, leaving space for possible exceptions.

What happens if a person who is not the owner of an immovable property rent it? Can he do it?

At first, he can only dispose of his own good, as any owner can do. He is attributed the right of usufruct, he can take advantage of the possible fruits that this property can generate.

But this right of usufruct can be trespassed to a third person, even to a fourth one, fifth, sixth, whatever is expressed at the moment of the right cession or trespassing.

The cession of right to usufruct of a property to another person can be done not only by renting contract. The cession can also be done by a loan agreement (loan of use) or by a term sale. It is enough that it was expressly included in the body of the document to have immediate effects.

Watch out this. It is not the same to trespass the right of loan, than the right of usufruct. They are very different things. The right of use is trespassed only, by a leasing contract when it is expressly forbidden to under lease.

It is only allowed the lessee to use the property for a specific object that it is stated in the contract, maybe a family house, commercial use, or any other. The right of usufruct is trespassed by means of a leasing contract, when it is mentioned specifically in the contract, that is to say when the lessee is facilitated to under lease.

It has to be expressly stated in the body of the contract. It is useless to be merely suggested. It has to be explained clearly and precisely.

In order the leasing contract has full force and legal validity, it is important that the person to be the lessee can demonstrate his capacity to do it. This capacity is granted by different ways, and not only by being the property right holder. A lessee can under lease, becoming in lessee of his lessor and at the same time, lessor of his under lessee.

We have to take into account the following element.

As the leasing contract is not a document susceptible of being registered in an office of immovable property registry, the contracting parts have not got the same security and trust that in the previous cases, and it can appear, in fact every day appears, new situations, dozens of possible situations against the actual laws.

We can meet situations in which the lessor, being at the same time the lesser, have not the faculty of under leasing, and he try to do it all the same. In the underworld of the real state business, this kind of scams abound.

It also happens that the commoners or members of a society, when they cannot materially sell their property to get his part, they decide to rent it on their own without the expressed authorization of the rest of co-owners. This represents a serious problem for the intermediators, that is to say, the agents. This is the reason we make emphasis on this question for the reader be clear when he intermediates in a possible leasing contract, where he is standing.

As they do not have the security and trust of the immovable property registry, the agents have to try to be tremendously exhaustive in these questions when they take part in them. It is necessary to be convinced of the negotiation can be made without risks for the lessee; in any case he will be the most complicated.

To lease a property without having the right to do it is a scam. That is why we call your attention particularly in this aspect.

3. - PURCHASER

The purchaser is the person who wants to buy the property. We cannot add very much. We can only say that as all the previous cases, it must be a person with legal capacity to contract, in the sense that he must not be under-aged, neither being legally disabled to contract. Under-aged people are not forbidden to buy properties, but they can do it through their legal representatives, or at least that they are emancipated.

4. - LESSEE OR HOUSEHOLDERS

They are those people that lease a property for its use and enjoyment. All the previous suppositions are also valid for them.

FRANKLIN DÍAZ

CHAPTER 7

METHODS OF CLIENTS ATTRACTION

We reach the point we can answer the following questions:

Where do we find clients?

Where can we find people who sell, buy or lease properties?

How do we create a clients portfolio?

As everything we want to achieve in life, we have to look for a method, a plan, a procedure to reach it.

There are some people who do not need to look for clients because they arrive by themselves. They just do it with the location of their activity, that is to say, a very well located headquarters where clients' fluency is produced spontaneously. This is the dreamed situation of any businessmen; that his clients come alone and effortlessly.

However, this is not the usual case but the exceptions. The agents have to manage to find their clients, and as consequence, the source of income.

There are dozens of methods to attract clients.

Citaremos aquí solo algunas de las más importantes:

We will quote some of them, the most important ones:

1. - PRESS: THE ADVERTISING WORLD IN NEWSPAPERS.

2. - LEAFLETS AND FLYERS

3. - INTRAPERSONAL RELATIONSHIPS.

4. - INTERNET: AN OPEN WINDOOW TO THE WORLD OF REAL STATE BUSINESS.

5. - "PURE AND HARD" SALES TECHNIQUE: THE "COLD DOOR" SELLER.

PRESS: ADVERTISING IN NEWSPAPERS

It is a method that consists of verifying daily throughout the different newspapers of the town where we live, or from where we consider doing the real states business, the press advertising in which the owners offer their respective properties.

These ads are majority found in the classifieds section.

This is a very useful method in big cities, where the real estate business is very strong.

Once we observe some of these advertisements from "lonely announcers", we call them to contact them to offer our services. It is so simple as to ask if he is interested in that an enterprise or a person specialized in these matters, get holds of everything that requires selling or leasing his property. From looking for the client that he demands, till the management of all the required documents.

Some people are used to trying the "White lies" technique here. It consists of saying to the seller or lessor, that they are interested in their property because they have "clients in his portfolio" ready to buy it or rent it, but in order to take them to see the property, it is necessary to sign a contract before by means of which they compromise to leave their property in exclusivity to be only them, and not other people, who sell it or leas it.

This is a very useful way to hook clients in big cities, where there is a fierce competence.

If the seller and/or a lessor bite the hook, the agent guarantees himself, at least, an interview with him. In this date he will not take the supposed client, that allegedly have waiting, but the contract of exclusiveness to be signed. Once it is signed, he will have the property in portfolio, and he can advertise it and promote it on his own account.

This is a kind of cheating, but a cheating with no intention of cause any damage, but to obtain a possible profit.

LEAFLEATS AND FLYERS

It consists of the elaboration of advertisements in which we offer our services as state agents.

What must they say?

The way it should be written depends on the chosen style. In this aspect we can say…

We suggest the following:

Do you want to sell or lease your immovable property?

Expert professionals are at your disposition to offer the best services in the real-estate market.

Please call or visit our place and you will check it.

(We attach our address, mail, and website and telephone numbers)

When we find an immovable property that it is offered by a lonely owner, and we do not have the opportunity to contact him, or by any other reason we are not able to do it, we simple leave one of these leaflets under their door, or we send it by any other means (neighbors, friends, relatives, etc.)

It is a usual practice of any state agents to capture some building porters and residential complexes. They offer a commission in exchange of information of immovable properties they know that are for sale or rent, or for helping in the distribution of the leaflets in their respective buildings and/or residential complexes.

It is often said that nobody is better than the porters to know the life of the neighborhood. We can also introduce leaflets into newspapers, preferably the days of more circulation (Sundays and holidays), or place them at the bus stops, public billboards at supermarkets, gas stations, or other places of mass stream of public.

There are enterprises or privates that dedicate to "leaflet activity", that is, to distribute leaflet and/or advertising, whether giving them in hand to passersby or putting them on the windscreen of cars for the drivers forced to see them and take them away. Many people believe that this method does not work, bit experience says the opposite.

In publicity matters there is a fundamental motto: "What it is not exhibited, is not sold".

INTERPERSONAL RELATIONSHIPS

It does not care how lonely e person can be, or the friends he has, there is always an owner likely to make any operations with his property within his social circle. We can also find people who have got immovable properties which they can lease, sell or exchange for another ones, but they do not dare to do it because they are afraid, lazy or simply because their lack of knowledge.

There we have to act the agents. This is a permanent and stable source of clients.

We have to make us identified with the activity, or at least, make us known in our surroundings, that we are dedicating, or we think to do it in a near future, to the exercise of the real-estate agency.

We always have to have at hand, in our handbags, pockets of our shirts, wherever we can quickly find them, an INTRODUCTION CARD.

An introduction card must have the necessary data. The simpler the better. It must have name, under it should be placed the expression "State Agent", or a similar one that identifies us with the job we are doing (for example, realtor; real estate broker, buying and selling and leasing of immovable properties, etc.)

It is not advisable to recharge the card of introduction with too much information, as for example, writing the social nets sites such as facebook, twitter, or others similar.

In an introductory card of our immovable activity, we only have to write the indispensable information to be contacted, and the social nets as much, the address of the blog or website in which we promote our products, our job. Nothing else.

Let's think what it is about "to attract clients", not to establish social relationships. Here we welcome social relations if they are useful to our purposes. Everything else is dispersion, and it is not of our interest.

INTERNET: AN OPEN WINDOW TO THE WORLD OF THE IMMOVABLE PROPERTY BUSSINESS

There is a multitude of portals, from the major to minor relevance, dedicated to the world of Immovable business.

Since those people who dedicate exclusively to this activity, till the ones who include it among his options.

We must remember that the use and access to internet is not equal in every part of the world. This aspect is very important to take it account. There are many countries and/or towns in which the use of internet is not a useful resource for this activity. It is more useful to pass the information from mouth to mouth and interpersonal relations.

In Spain, just to mention two cases, we have the portal "idealista.com" and "fotocasa.es" as examples of successful portals in the immovable advertising online.

In both cases, the access is free previous registration. Anyone can publish there what they sell or rent, they can attach photographs, videos, plans, addresses, conditions, prices, and the whole spectrum of additional specificity that contribute to a better description of the product offered.

Besides, we have also got a multitude of webs dedicated to the advertising world, on line, most of them free. "milanuncios.com" and "segundamano.es" are other possibilities in Spain. There you can also publish the properties to sell or rent, although without the possibility to make so much specification compared to the portals with exclusive dedication to the immovable business. It seems logical, of course.

The world of business in internet has multiplied so much, that just to write in a search engine (Google, Msn, Bing, etc.) the expression

"Publish advertising" you find dozens and dozens of webs dedicated to the business of free advertising online.

There resides a source, a fount of possible clients. It is just a question of contact them timely by mail or by telephones the sellers published in order to be contacted.

Many people will say that if they have published on their own ad of the apartment that sell or rent, it is because they are not interested that an intermediate person work for him. It is not always true, and it is a way of interposing a "previous excuse" for not looking for our so anxious "Holy Grail": the clients' portfolio.

What do you know about the personal circumstances of who publishes on his own to speculate about it? Nothing! And that is the reason we do not try. This is what people do every day in most countries who dedicate to the immovable business: look for clients.

Maybe, that this first contact that we dislike a priori has been the possibility to meet the better of our clients.

Why do we think that the person who we are calling is waiting anxiously someone to help him to sell or rent his property; "or that" he has just live through a traumatic situation in his life that avoid dedicating time a effort to sell or rent his property "or that" he has just won the lottery and he is not longer interested in working anymore and our call comes in the best moment; "or that" he has to travel to a foreign country during which it would be great that someone helps him to collocate his property; "or that" he has just became disable as a result of a bad temporal illness; "or positive thats" we can go to, instead of thinking negatively, pessimistic ideas. In any case, a "NO" is an answer before we try a contact looking for a "YES".

We can always put our ad in solitary in the portal of immovable and/or of classified advertising, asking immovable for sail and/or rent. Remember what we have already said about the leaflets contents.

Thus, a good ad in search of immovable properties could say: Prestige Enterprise dedicated to the real-estate market ask immovable properties on sale and for rent in the (...............) zone. Clients waiting

And we put our address, our blog or a promoting web, telephone number and mail.

"PURE AND HARD" SALES TECHNIQUE: THE "COLD DOOR" SELLER"

The title of this section gives us the idea of what this technique imply; the lonely sale, face to face meeting with a stranger who needs to convince, the art of seduction in its highest expression.

Somebody who belongs to the religious branch of the so called "Jehovah Witnesses" would be an excellent "cold door" seller. I have never known anybody so insistent.

In this case it is about to contact directly with the person that sells or rent their properties. When we see that there is a "on sale" or "for rent" signs we call directly to the door where they are, and we face with the possible client out of doubts.

We will try firmly but tactful to find some weak points with certain determination to introduce ourselves to discover possible spaces in which we can start the seduction attack.

For example, we should see the objects of the house to detect the owner's favorite soccer team, his preferences, if he is married, with children, if he is religious, etc.

We need something to be our starting point, a topic to begin our conversation, a "detail" to break the ice, a way to gain confidence.

This is the technique used for those who guess your future through the reading of cards on television late at night. They are not but natural seducers. Everything they are saying is what they get form the same interlocutor, from a previous chat before passing the call to the presenter, or by the same presenter when talking with him on air. While he does it, he is asking the caller subtle questions, almost imperceptible, whose answers he is joining according to what the caller wants to hear. Then, all this summoned information, together with a series of generalities that are equal to everyone, the presenter will predict his future.

The fool will believe it and he will turn his life towards what the alleged fortune teller has said. With the passing of time and the fulfilled prophesy, he would attribute his achievements to the guessing of that night, and not to have followed his efforts unconsciously, to the consecution of these goals.

He does not realize that the only thing he did was to program him. It is as simple as that.

The person, who is able to convince other person, has won the world; the planet earth is at his feet. He is person who never suffers needs, because he will get everything he wants on his own, through strategies of seduction, persuasion and convincing.

A teacher of sales I met during my preparation told me a phrase in one occasion, which marked me for life:

"There is no such Word as "¡No!" for a good seller". A professional seller change a "NO" into a "YES", and this is when he starts selling. This is the indicator that his career starts; this is the sign to develop his arts of seduction, of charming, enchantment, falling in love."

We cannot "attempt" to all the people in the same way. It is necessary to have in mind something so obvious as to know that every human being is different and some of them are "very different". Consequently, it depends on the person we are dealing; it will be our behavior, our attitude in front of him.

It is necessary to make our own qualification, starting with some psychological schemes very used at marketing school. We need "to know" human beings.

MEETING THE HUMANS

We, Human beings are very different from one another. By this time of the development of humanity, and consequently, the evolution of science, and among them psychological sciences that study our personalities, we are lucky to know that there are a series of patterns or models where each of us can fit in.

Although many people want to differentiate from the rest, the human species has certain determined natural characteristics.

Yet when it is true that each individual is unique and unrepeatable, it is also true that all of us have a series of distinctive features that delimit us, and let us be classified in determined individualized groups.

It is said that every human being, without exception, has three forms of "I" within.

Namely:

1. - The father "I"

2. - The adult "I"

3. - The child "I"

When we say that all of us have this forms of "I" we refer to "EVERYBODY", from the newly born baby, to the oldest person on earth.

Let's see what these "forms of I" are about.

1. - The father "I" is our inner part that represents protection, the strength, repression, aggression, jealousy, power. That is a fearless person that considers everything has got a solution.

2. - The adult "I" is our inner part that represents the mature, reflexive, analytical, methodical and ordered being. It is the part that looks for a reasonable solution to all problems, thought and reflexive.

3. - And finally, the child "I" who can be afraid, shy, weepy and frightened.

The "I" part that press upon the rest will be the one to determine our personality, our behavior.

The person who has the father "I" will be a strong, dared, aggressive and violent person. A bossy and conductive person likes to be initiative, and wants to take control of the situation.

The person, who has more developed his adult "I", will be a person you can think with, to talk to, because he will have a well marked rational personality, mature, coherent, reflexive.

Finally, the one who has his personality developed around his child "I" will be a person with a stressed childish and immature character. He is a person who does not like complications, who likes to have things done by another.

What we do as human beings among ourselves is to relate, to link through communication.

The part of our "I" that influence upon us is decisive at the time of establishing relations with another person.

If we have more of our father "I", we will like to be treated more like them, that people subordinate to us, to be obeyed, to be recognized, respect and submission.

If we have more of our adult "I", we will feel very alike with those who dialogue, think, reflect with ourselves.

And finally, if we have more of our "child I", we feel more alike when we are treated like children. We will like to be spoiled, and protected.

What is the use of all this information to a state agent?

It is very simple. We start from this knowledge, of interrelation, and through it we reach the proposed objectives. A person that knows how to treat another has many advantages at the time to negotiate. He will know how to behave with him, how to convince him, how to gain his empathy, and consequently his generosity. He will have an important track ahead when taking him to his land.

CHAPTER 8

MARKETING TECHNIQUES

What is marketing?

Marketing is usually defined as a group of techniques to achieve the trading of a determined product.

We have already said in many occasions that The Real Estate Agents are more than simple sellers. We sell "something". This something is a profitable product.

Which is our product?

We sell houses, farms, apartments… NO! These are not our products. Our product is our activity, our management. This is the object of our payment. This is where we obtain our profit.

We as sellers, need to have clear some notions and basic strategies of selling; a series of useful tips to sell any kind of products. They are useful for a vacuum cleaners seller and for The Real Estate Agent.

1. - LOVE FOR SELLING

The sale is a process conceived as an act to convince other to buy something. It is a process of self-realization in certain way. We feel self-realized when we sell something, when we convince somebody to buy something we offer. We feel an immense satisfaction when we achieve an object we have proposed; besides the sensation of obtaining a good profit at the same time.

Maybe, that we do not feel love for selling while we do not perceive the achievements. But take it for granted that things start changing as soon as you can see the results.

You start learning more about selling, how to seduce, about how to gain more and more clients, and as a consequence, more and more money. What happiness!

A good seller is a natural seducer. A good seller is a person that can bring out in his client the need for what he is offering, and not only that, but also to show the possible alternatives to buy it.

An example of my own experience would be illustrative for this point.

In one occasion, I entered a motorcycle selling concessionaire with my twelve year old daughter. We were not interested in buying a motorcycle; we came in casually on our way. I had never ridden a motorcycle in my life and we were just looking. The seller, a smart young boy, came to me to ask my opinion of the motorcycles, if I liked them. I told him that they very nice. Then he asked me to sit on one of them, the one I liked it most. He also told me that I imagined the breeze on my face while the girls watched me ride along the avenue with trees. I smiled and answer that I could imagine it but I did not have motorcycle driving license, neither experience. He told me that with my car driving license was enough. And he also told me that my lack of experience was not an obstacle, they could teach me some free motorcycle driving classes. I told him that I had no money, and he said that was not a problem, that he would do the financing.

I was silent some minutes, and he said that he would not hurried me, he was only interested in selling, but if I was willing to buy there would not be any problem.

Before leaving me alone, he told me that he could give me one concessionaire motorcycle to use it for some days without any compromise, or that I would assist to have driving classes whenever I wanted. It was not necessary to buy one. He also said that if I preferred I could consult with my wife and the rest of the family. I told him I was a widower and that my only family was my daughter, who was there with me. He told me to think if I deserved or not the pleasure of riding the motorcycle. After that, he also told me that he would not say anything else, that the rest was my business.

After that, he went to his office and left me alone with my thoughts. My daughter who was paying attention to the conversation, told me to do what I consider convenient. She realized that I was in doubt.

The smart seller, not only had he showed me the virtues of buying a motorcycle, but also he had touched my psychological fiber. He brought up a need in me that I had not before: to ride a motorcycle.

I went out waving goodbye to the seller. I thought that although the offer was tempting; I was not willing to meet problems. However, the following days I dreamt several times with I was told by the seller; that I was riding my motorbike along a wide avenue with trees, and some girls smiled while I was passing by.

Two months later, I bought the motorcycle. There were not girls smiling at my riding; but I did ride on motorcycle along the avenues of my city.

2. - KNOWLEDGE OF THE PRODUCT TO SELL

If you do not know well what you sell, you are irreparably condemned to failure. We have to know very well the product you sell.

We have already said repeatedly that our product is intermediation, human service; our disposition to manage the requirements for the immovable business in question.

Our offer implies the disposition of our clients of a presumed knowledge that we must have about the immovable section. Since then it is "indispensable" to keep up to date with the knowledge of prices fluctuations in the immovable trading; the mortgage interests; the requirements to contract a mortgage; the services prices (water, light, gas, community); commissions charged by the real-estate of the competence; the tenant legislation.

Any knowledge we can acquire and/or have at hand in the practice of our job will not be enough. It is very important to keep us up at date.

How do you acquire this knowledge?

Practicing

Each management we make, each business we close, will be useful to increase the knowledge we need.

The theoretical foundation is always necessary and indispensable. When you do not know anything, investigate, ask, and consult. Even more, although much theory we study, nothing can replace the knowledge which is acquired day after day from experience.

3. - KEEP UP TO DATE WITH THE PRICES OF THE IMMOVABLE TRADING

After certain time of practice, The Real Estate Agent should be able to determine, for better or for worse, the average price to rent or sell a property located in his zone of influence.

This ability arises spontaneously as a consequence of the daily comparison of immovable properties with others, and by getting familiar with the trade in which we work.

It also happens with seller of used cars, with the passing of time he learns to determine the value of a car in a determined moment with the only data of brand, model and its general state.

A state agent must be able to calculate the Price for selling or renting an immovable by having a look at it, independently of the real price. There are enterprises and professionals that they only dedicate to this activity, to make valuations. The valuations that a state agent does do not have to be a technical. Their estimations of a trading price are based on what they are demanding on average to the owners for the sale or rent of their properties, and also for what the trading of clients are ready to pay.

4. - BE ONESELF

The Real Estate Agent, is in his seller facet of cold door, must show himself as he actually is without masks. It happens that when we make a cold door contact and we meet the possible new client, he will detect intuitively our costumes and he will pay us with the same coin, wearing another costume. So, what is funny?

We could not convince anybody of anything, neither enter his "Interior I" because he will be wearing his costume, like us. What we have started, instead of a possible fructiferous negotiation, will be a cheating game that will not give us any profit.

Although, if we intend sincerity, we will stimulate in him a similar answer, that is what we really want.

Thus, nobody will cheat anybody. Besides, it is not necessary.

5. - SINCERE GREETING AND CORDIAL SMILE

Both things are essential once we have made visual contact with our possible new client. Nobody can reject a smile. A cordial and sincere smile contributes strongly to start any conversation, about any negotiation.

Politicians use this resource in their electoral campaigns. It is very difficult, almost impossible, to meet future voters with ugly face. Smile is a good presentation card.

6. - ATTRACT ATTENTION, INTEREST AND DESIRE:

It is fundamental to attract attention, the interest of the client in our person.

If "our sincere greeting and cordial smile" are not helping to stimulate the attention of our possible client, there are some tricks we can use.

Let's see:

a) Let's ask him a simple question.

b) Let's make a surprising affirmative statement.

c) Let's say an enigmatic phrase.

d) Let's introduce a small symbolic present.

e) Hagamos referencia a un cliente o amigo suyo.

f) Usemos un cumplido sincero y admirativo.

f) Let's make a sincere and admiring compliment.

g) Let's give him a piece of a recently news we know he is interested in.

h) Let's make a useful and discrete suggestion.

On the other hand, we can also follow these advices about "the interest and desire" of our client:

a) Let's make a brief demonstration, pencil in hand, presenting figures and convincing results.

b) Let's dramatize the advantages and looses that he would have if he does not make use of our services.

c) Let's present them testimonies of clients satisfied with our services, giving proofs, if necessary.

d) Let's watch carefully his body language, adapting our arguments to what we are discovering.

e) Let's look for his conviction, briefly and clearly, working upon his key arguments; which they are sum up to "HOW HE WILL GET PROFIT OF OUR SERVICES, OF OUR MANAGEMENT."

f) Let's provide conformity with our documents to our future client; with the true fact that he lacks the advantages of our job, our management; and we insist in a reliable way, that us, and ONLY US, can give him these pieces of advantage.

g) Let's evoke in him, our words, images that place him enjoying the benefits of our mediation. When using this technique, let's try to consider the affective, sentimental feeling side of our hypothetic future client.

7. - PRONOUNCE THE NAME OR SURNAME OF THE CLIENT FREQUENTLY.

Our names are the sweetest sounds we can listen from other lips. This detail is very well known by the negotiators in hostage situations; the call center attendants (the first thing they do is introducing themselves and ask us our name to speak to us in first person); politicians in conferences (they are used to calling journalists by their name); etc.

It seems foolish, but psychological speaking, to listen to our name in several times and in different occasions by the same person while talking has a strong positive effect.

It is a way to start taming the wild beast.

8. - BE EFFECTIVE LISTENER

Human beings, as affective beings that we are actually are, have an immense need to be flattered. It can be done applying the advice described above. You can adopt different ways, from the simple repetition of their name or surname, till the compliment and the sincere praise.

Besides, there is a very effective way to flatter somebody without he realizes it. If we break the ice and enter his interior world; the one we need so much to manipulate for achieving our goals: This is the "art" of listening.

In an interview, we must try to listen better than speaking. We must try our first words to stimulate the client desire to speak, to say things. Once this first objective is achieved, we must listen carefully, paying attention to everything that our possible client wants to say. We must not interrupt or distract him while talking.

It is not about to wear a mask of the "good listener". We must not think the things we are going to say when it is our turn, losing our concentration in what our possible client is saying. We will speak when it is necessary but we have already won the attention and trust of the client because we have given the best psychological present: the art of listening.

9. - WE MUST BE CONSCIOUS OF OUT LIMITS

While being state agents, we are dealing with explosive material, that is to say, we are dealing with subjects that there is a lot to say. The immovable sector includes a lot of human feelings, from the material aspect to the strictly affective and emotive. We are talking about objects that have the quality of feeling differently in people.

It is not correct to presume of "smarties", of "wise people". Because the same property can be seen differently depending on who is watching it. We do not see an apartment to sell in the same way the family who lived in it during years or generations. It represents money to quantify for us, but for them it represents memories, habits, affections, etc. We should not give our opinion about these subjects because we are not experts on them. The only experts in feelings at the time of leaving an immovable property are their owners.

We must not presume about our knowledge about the property business, because although we know enough about it there is always someone that knows more than us.

This the important reason for which we have pointed out that idea in the previous paragraphs, about trying to get as much information as we can about our possible client, before starting negotiation with him. The more information the better, to know who we are working with and which are our limits in the matter.

10. - WE HAVE TO ADMIT VALID OBJECTIONS.

Some objections to our job cannot be rejected because they are irrefutable, certain and authentic.

Let's pay honor to our clients accepting them, and if it is possible, let's congratulate for their arguments. Then we remark, that such objections are compensated by the service we offer. You must notice that we do not say that the objections are not certain, true, but "are compensated" by other things.

The main profit of accepting an objection as valid leaves a possible client impressed by our sincerity and frankness. And this is priceless.

11. - DO NOT USE THE EXPRESSION: "YES, BUT..."

The person who invented the expression "Yes, but..." was not a psychologist, and much less was a seller.

The word "but" is like a pomegranate about to explode. It produces the immediate sensation of confrontation, of struggling, of combating, of contradiction, of starting conflict. It is a word that chills out cordiality, and generates antagonism, willingness to refute, and paralyzed the persuasive process.

It is much effective, soft and cordial the conjunction "y..." Let's see an example:

If the client says;

<<I think the commission is too high>>

It is not the same this answer:

<<Yes, but we are a serious and responsible enterprise, you will be benefited because (bla, bla, bla...)>>

Than:

<<Yes, and we are a serious and responsible, so you will be benefited because (bla, bla, bla...) >>

In the first answer you confront, while in the second one there is continuity, balance, and calm.

12. - CLOSING RECOMMENDATIONS

When we have the sensation that the business is almost closed, do not waste time, and act according these pieces of advice:

a) Ask the client directly to take a decision.

b) Never lose confidence in that our client will answer our asking.

c) Keep in mind an important argument on our side, still not said in case the client is in doubt till the last minute.

d) Keep in mind a important question for the last push.

e) Let's get the client say "YES" about anything. Meanwhile more times he assesses the better. It is a way of letting down barriers in his mind.

f) Never give up.

g) Do not charge too much tension on the last phase.

h) If the client doubts, let's appeal to a client witness who has good relation with us.

i) Let's take out the pen in the proper moment. If you do it before the right time, it frightens, if you do it after, it induces to very dangerous final reflections.

j) Try your best for the client find much more difficult to refuse than to accept.

k) Once we have achieved what we want, let's go away immediately! Do not waste time. Thus we avoid dangerous reflections that could end up our reached objective.

We have explained many things so far, actions to perform, the way we must act. Even the things we should never do, and these things we also have to know.

Some things we should never do in our labor of attracting clients are the followings:

a) We do not have to begin sentences with an excuse (Excuse me, I was passing by and…", or: "Sorry, I saw your "for rent" poster and…")

b) Never compel the client to shake hands with us. Let's give them to take the initiative.

c) Keep up a reasonable close physical distance with the client, without invading his inner space, intimate zone.

d) We must not smoke in presence of the client, if he does not smoke.

e) Do not start contact with a joke, unless it is on our behalf.

f) Never talk to our client about our difficulties, of our problems.

CHAPTER 9

THE EARNINGS: THE FRUIT OF STATE AGENT LABOR

The Real Estate Agent profits obtained from his job are not usually regulated. His activity is not similar to an ordinary clerk. Although it is certain that if you work for another person things are very different, because in this case you should have a stated salary.

The job of state agent is a very liberal one. Any people can do this work; we have already said it in the previous chapters. You only require disposition. The Real Estate Agent usually agrees previously with the immovable owner/householder the price to be paid by his job. This agreement, due it is law between the parts must be respected. It is of compulsory fulfillment, and consequently it can be demanded at court in case of breaking it.

Which are the limits of this agreement?

The ones established between the parts.

We have also commented in the previous chapters that the only limit a contract has is the limit established by law. Everything that is not forbidden, it is allowed.

The parts can agree their free will the amount they want to set as profit for The Real Estate Agent in any business they do.

However, the use and practice of this activity, has become in the uses and customs very extended in the world. They are not the only way to establish gains, but they are what they have already said: "Very extended uses and customs".

According to them, there are two of the ways mostly used to establish the price The Real Estate Agent is going to obtain by his services.

1. - Percentage

2. - Overcharge price

It will depend on the operation strategy, whether it is a sale or a renting.

Let's see both cases separately.

SALES:

Regarding sales, the gains are fixed in this way.

1. – Percentage:

It consists of determining a percentage upon the sale Price to be paid by the purchaser.

For example, it is determined that the gain perceived by The Real Estate Agent for his work will be of 5% of the sale value, and the property is sold in 100.000€, his gain will be of 5.000€.

2. - Overcharge:

It consists of establishing The Real Estate Agent gain will be the difference between the effective paid by the purchaser, and the previously agreed price between The Real Estate Agent and the seller.

For example, if it is agreed that the sale price for the seller will be 100.000€, and The Real Estate Agent could sell it by 120.000€. The gain for his work will be of 20.000€.

LEASSING:

In the leasing matters, we have to distinguish two situations; the act of renting in itself, and the administration of the rented property.

In the first case, the act of renting in itself, the gains are obtained directly from the lesser, not from the lessor.

You get the equivalent to a month rent in concept of "administrative expenses". Some people call it a month of commission".

In this way, the lesser, besides the months he has to deposit for bail of the immovable (usually two) and/or the month that has to pay in advance, another month will be added for the management of the immovable property.

In the second case, that is, in case that the immovable manager assumes the administration of the rented property too (collect the rents and pay them month by month to the lessor in his bank account), the gains use to be agreeing as common agree with the lessor, having the following modes:

1. - Percentage

2. - Overcharge

1. - Percentage

It is about to fix a percentage rate upon the amount to pay by monthly for by the lessor, which will be used The Real Estate Agent by the factor his management,

For example, if a lessor pay every month the amount of 600€, and it is determined that The Real Estate Agent will get every month 10% for his intervention, the quantity that will bear will be 60€ a month.

2. - Overcharge

In this case it determines that what it will get The Real Estate Agent for his intermediation will be the difference between the previously agreed price with the client-lessor, and the effective cancelled final quantity by the lesser.

For example, if it is agreed between The Real Estate Agent and the owner lessor that the property is rented that the immovable is going to be rented in 600€, and The Real Estate Agent can hire for 700€, the perceived amount by the last will be of 100€ monthly.

FINAL CONSIDERATION OF THE SECOND PART OF THIS BOOK

Once it is seen and learnt the basic aspect that there must be known in order to work in the immovable intermediation, the only aspects to be learnt and managed are the themes corresponding to an elaboration and management of the immovable contracts.

For this situation I have elaborated a complete text with the forms that are needed to work in this section, and it constituted a second part of this work. This book is actually a sum up of contracts and forms to work in Spain. That is the reason for which it is not included in this book. It was conceived to exercise in any country of the world, taking into account the specific differences of each. The attached Annexes of contracts are only specific for Spain.

If you are a Spanish reader and you are interested in buying, you can do it in any distribution platform of digital books with the following name: The Real Estate Agent job (II) (CONTRACTS and FORMS)

Printed in Great Britain
by Amazon